The Real Estate Agent's Guide to FSBOs

The Real Estate Agent's Guide to FSBOs

Make Big Money Prospecting For-Sale-By-Owner Properties

John Maloof

AMACOM
American Management Association
New York • Atlanta • Brussels • Chicago • Mexico City • San Francisco
Shanghai • Tokyo • Toronto • Washington, D. C.

Special discounts on bulk quantities of AMACOM books are available to corporations, professional associations, and other organizations. For details, contact Special Sales Department, AMACOM, a division of American Management Association, 1601 Broadway, New York, NY 10019. Tel: 212-903-8316. Fax: 212-903-8083.
E-mail: specialsls@amanet.org
Website: www.amacombooks.org/go/specialsales
To view all AMACOM titles go to: www.amacombooks.org

This publication is designed to provide accurate and authoritative information in regard to the subject matter covered. It is sold with the understanding that the publisher is not engaged in rendering legal, accounting, or other professional service. If legal advice or other expert assistance is required, the services of a competent professional person should be sought.

REALTOR® is a registered collective membership mark that identifies a real estate professional who is a member of the National Association of REALTORS® and subscribes to its strict Code of Ethics. AMACOM uses these names throughout this book in initial capital letters or ALL CAPITAL letters for editorial purposes only, with no intention of trademark violation.

Library of Congress Cataloging-in-Publication Data
Maloof, John.
  The real estate agent's guide to FSBOs : make big money prospecting for-sale-by-owner properties / John Maloof.
    p. cm.
  Includes bibliographical references and index.
  ISBN-13: 978-0-8144-0043-2
  ISBN-10: 0-8144-0043-4
  1. House selling. 2. Real property. I. Title.

HD1379.M357   2008
333.33'83—dc22

2007012817

Printing number
10 9 8 7 6 5 4 3 2 1

Contents

Contents

Acknowledgments

I want to thank all of those people whose influential books and training sessions sculpted me into the salesperson I am today. Tom Hopkins, Earl Nightingale, Brian Tracy, and Tony Robbins—you are highly regarded as the mentors behind my success.

To all of my past and present clients, you have given me the privilege of serving you. I am thankful for the experience of knowing and learning the ropes from such a wonderful group of people, most of which are now my friends.

The Real Estate Agent's
Guide to FSBOs

Introduction

The platform is waiting for you. Will you take it? Or will you give it to someone else? Each one of us possesses the will to make it to the top of whatever it may be that we wish to explore. In this book I open up a new door for agents who would like to take their career to new heights in an area that is an abundant resource that has been largely untapped. If you don't take advantage of it, someone else will. This resource is the For Sale By Owner, or FSBO.

The purpose of this book is to help agents discover a new successful approach to selling real estate—through FSBOs.

What You Will Get from This Book

Did you know that, according to the National Association of Realtors®, 86 percent of new real estate agents don't make it past the first year in this business? That's right. The majority of new agents give up due to the frustration and overwhelming start-up costs involved in this industry from the very beginning. Little do they know that a simple key to success lies right under their nose and often right next door.

Now that you're a real estate agent, what do you do now . . . hope that business comes to you? If this is so, you're in for a rude awakening. It is possible to market yourself broke without even a single prospect call. You can contact your "sphere of influence" and hope someone that you know is buying or selling sometime soon. Even if you get one sale, it's not enough to survive. Instead of throwing mud at the wall and hoping it will stick, get out there and work for your money because if *you* don't, *others* will.

What if I told you that you don't need years of experience in this industry to make as much as the pros? What if I told you that you can make a six-figure income without knowing anyone to get referrals from? Now that I have your attention, I can tell you that it's true . . . *you can!* Not only is it possible, but I did it myself, and I did it my very first year in the business.

In my first year as a real estate agent I had over forty transactions. That's equivalent to over $12 million in real estate sales. I also did this without hiring an assistant. For the first time in my life I made a six-figure income. That year I won four awards: two from Century 21 and two from the Chicago Association of Realtors. This paved the way for my future success in this business.

What if I told you that in my first year as an agent I was

only twenty-three years old? In my first year in real estate, I lived with my mother in a small apartment in Chicago. I hardly had any dress clothes, and I had a sub-par automobile. I'm sure you would think someone like this wouldn't have much luck in a business that relies largely on first impressions.

The point I am trying to make is that even with all of this against me, I still made a six-figure income selling real estate. And I did it solely by working FSBOs. Can you imagine how much I could have made if I had a nice car, new dress clothes, and was well presented? If I made a six-figure income at the age of 23 under those circumstances, then *anyone can!* As sales started to accrue I invested in my image and presentation. Sale after sale, I climbed my way up the ladder of success.

As I have been teaching FSBO classes and coaching new and experienced agents about how to make money in the FSBO market, I realized the demand to get the word out. What I lay out in this book are not theories or ideas, but proven techniques to succeed in listing and selling FSBOs. These techniques are presented here for you to digest and implement into your own action plan. This is not written as a motivational book, although it does contain some motivational tactics to give your career the push it deserves.

As an effort not to flood you with do's and don'ts, I purposely kept this book short and to the point. I would recommend, however, that after you finish reading this book in its entirety, that you read many of the important chapters in this book a second time, and that you keep it on hand as a quick reference guide.

Whom This Book Will Benefit

All agents, new and experienced, shall find that this book will open doors to new career possibilities. FSBOs have always existed, it's just that many agents were never trained on how to effectively approach and utilize them.

For new agents, this book will serve as a no-nonsense foundation builder that can jump-start their careers virtually overnight. New agents especially, who normally find it hard to succeed without a referral base, may find that the techniques taught in this book can earn them a six-figure income their very first year. There is no hype. There are no seminars to attend. And, there are no software programs to purchase. You don't even have to work at the office. Work from home like I did and make the money that you once dreamed of.

This book is aimed at not just one level of real estate agent, but at every agent across the spectrum. Experienced agents will find that they always wanted to explore the FSBO market, but they never gave it the attention to really open up the potential. With the tools presented in this book, experienced agents will find that FSBOs will add an extra boost to their career.

I can't leave out the top producers. I am your testimonial. As a top producer, I focused on the techniques that are outlined in this book to make it possible. If you already are a top producer and you aren't giving the FSBO market attention . . . *wow!* You're going to have a great year once you incorporate the principles outlined in this book into your business.

Lastly, for all you brokers out there, this is an excellent book to give to all of your agents in order to build the office inventory and increase your company's potential. Help your office's positive image by letting your agents explore new avenues that will give them an edge.

Main Points

It often happens that too much information can make someone miss the main points. In order to keep you focused on the main points, when you've finished reading this book, brush up on the following chapters:

Chapter 3: FSBO Prospecting Plan
Chapter 5: The FSBO System
Chapter 6: FSBO Sales Techniques
Chapter 7: Special Telephone Techniques
Chapter 8: The FSBO Listing Presentation

The topics covered in these chapters are the backbone to making FSBOs an income gusher, but you need to know the whole picture before focusing on those specific points. So read up.

CHAPTER 1

The FSBO

Real integrity is doing the right thing, knowing that nobody's going to know whether you did it or not.

—OPRAH WINFREY

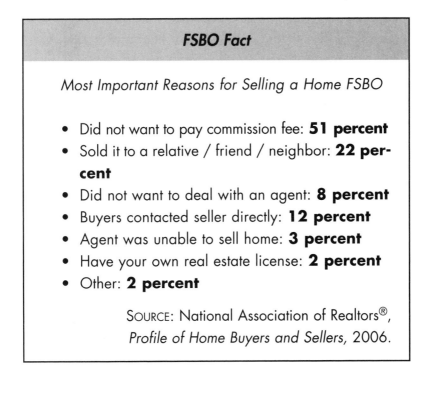

FSBO Fact

Most Important Reasons for Selling a Home FSBO

- Did not want to pay commission fee: **51 percent**
- Sold it to a relative / friend / neighbor: **22 percent**
- Did not want to deal with an agent: **8 percent**
- Buyers contacted seller directly: **12 percent**
- Agent was unable to sell home: **3 percent**
- Have your own real estate license: **2 percent**
- Other: **2 percent**

SOURCE: National Association of Realtors®, *Profile of Home Buyers and Sellers*, 2006.

Did you know that about nine out of ten For Sale By Owners (FSBOs) end up hiring an agent? You may wonder who these agents are that they end up hiring, because only 5 percent of agents actually work with FSBOs. These are by far the most abundant leads in this industry, yet the area is left wide open. *So, why aren't you working them?*

What Is a FSBO?

The "For Sale By Owner" (FSBO for short, and pronounced FIZ-BO) is a homeowner who tries to sell his or her home without a real estate agent involved. Typically, FSBOs ignore all the hazards, legal paperwork, and bottom-line business factors involved in selling a home. Therefore, many try selling by themselves because they don't know any better. Another reason many choose to sell themselves is that they may have had a bad experience with an agent in the past and find it hard to get over it. Then you have the FSBO who thinks she's got the magic touch and can do just as good a job as any agent, but as you and I both know, this couldn't be further from the truth.

For agents from all across the spectrum, new and experienced, the FSBO market is a resource that should not be overlooked. I am not going say too much more about what a FSBO is; if you have a real estate license you should know by now. But in this book I will go into depth about the work involved with making six figures solely by utilizing the FSBO market to your advantage. Please, if you aren't serious about trying some of the techniques taught in this book and implementing them, then put this book down now. It's not for you. If you are interested in going forward, however, you must understand that making six figures a year is not easy. It takes hard work, focus, determination, and the ability to learn from your mistakes. If you possess those characteristics, and are willing to accept these assignments, this will work for you.

Why Do We Need FSBOs?

One good thing about FSBOs is that you will always have them around. There will be FSBOs to tap into *at all times*. Best of all, you don't have to convince them to sell their home; their homes are already for sale. It is your job to convince FSBOs that what you offer will help them sell their home faster, easier, and, most importantly, get them top dollar.

I don't believe in exploiting FSBOs as vulnerable or weak, but instead I see working with FSBOs as an opportunity to help them down the right path. You see, we as real estate agents must maintain our image as, like Tom Hopkins calls us, "professional problem solvers." There are many agents, just like in any other industry, who look out only for themselves at the expense of innocent sellers and buyers. We must abide by ethics laws and agency regulations—not only because we have to, but because we should want to.

The reasons why we need FSBOs are numerous. Many new agents need to quickly find business in order to stay alive in this competitive industry, and FSBOs are the best resource for quick listings and sales. Over time these sales will lead to a referral-based business with less work required and, ultimately, more money to be made.

The FSBO seller is most often someone who doesn't understand how we as agents can help them sell their home. That is what we're here to do: Inform them about the honest benefits of using an agent and what they stand to gain by using one.

Why Do Sellers Go FSBO?

In order to fully understand FSBOs, you'll have to put yourself in their shoes. Ask yourself, why would someone decide to sell FSBO? The most common answer is, *to save on commissions*. According to the statistics from the National Association of Realtors® (NAR), which were cited at the beginning of the chapter, 51 percent of FSBOs said that commissions were the number one reason that convinced them to go it alone. There are other reasons as well, but this is the main concern that drove sellers to go FSBO. This reasoning is based solely on lack of knowledge of how marketing their home through an agent can benefit them. Many people have refinanced their home up to their eyeballs, and they need every penny that they can get out of the property in order to be able to pay off the bank. They may feel that in order to get top dollar, they need to sell their home without an agent. But the statistics are in favor of marketing with a professional in just about every circumstance—they just don't know that.

Now that you know that FSBO motivation #1 is to save money, we'll have to presume that when FSBO sellers decide to list their home with an agent they'll instantly lose some money from their bottom line because of real estate commissions . . . right? Well that's where it gets tricky. You see, most FSBOs expect to keep their bottom line the same even after they list with an agent. That would mean increasing the asking price to absorb some of the commission that they're going to have to pay. In this type of scenario, it's most likely that the seller will want to price the home over market value.

Unless you feel that the seller will reduce the price over time, an overpriced listing will only cost you time and money. So how do you combat the high asking price of most FSBOs? You must have your listing presentation nailed down. Accurate comparables containing sold and expired listings are the true tools for measuring market value. You also need to prove to the seller that they will be making more money by listing with a professional, even factoring in the brokerage fees. You'll need to outline this in black and white for them. When a seller lists with an agent they tend to make more at closing as opposed to selling FSBO. If you put it that way, they would be bending over backwards to list their home with an agent . . . *right?*

Why Sellers Go Broke Selling FSBO

In any business, selling a product or service requires three elements:

1. A product
2. A price
3. A shelf (or exposure)

FSBOs have the first two elements but lack the third and probably the most important one, *exposure*. How can you sell a product without a shelf to sell it on? You can't. That is the same as selling a home without market exposure. That is the realization many FSBOs eventually come to.

Here's the breakdown: When a home is marketed with an agent, it exposes the home to more buyers, which brings in more buyer traffic through the door. With more traffic through the door, the chances of selling will increase, which maximizes the sales price. For the information that backs this up visit the NAR website for the current years' statistics on selling FSBO vs. using an agent. In 2006, the NAR's study showed that selling a home with an agent will increase the sales price by 32 percent at closing as opposed to selling FSBO. That is a national average loss of $59,800 per FSBO by not using a Realtor. *This is astounding!*

I will be using this example throughout the book. It simply means that with an investment of a 5 percent brokerage fee, the seller can make a *640 percent return!* There is absolutely no investment today that offers that type of return. Take advantage of these research statistics in your presentations. Check out the most recent FSBO statistics in Appendix B and visit www.realtor.org/research.nsf/pages/fsbofacts.

CHAPTER 2

Understanding What It Takes

Remember, you only have to succeed the last time.

—Brian Tracy

FSBO Fact

Eighty-five percent of buyers said they were very satisfied with all aspects of their real estate agent's knowledge and expertise of the purchase process, and 82 percent were very satisfied with their agent's knowledge of the real estate market.

Source: National Association of Realtors®, *Profile of Home Buyers and Sellers*, 2005.

In order for you to understand what it takes to be a successful agent, you'll need the energy and motivation to take yourself to the next level. Just keep in mind that there is no such thing as a born salesperson. *Anyone* can sell real estate. *Anyone* can be successful at selling real estate. But not everyone *will* be successful at selling real estate. The reasons why most fail are many. More importantly, the reasons why some succeed are overpowering.

The common stereotype among many home sellers is that real estate agents are only looking out for one thing . . . *themselves.* This couldn't be further from the truth. A few bad seeds in the real estate industry can ruin the perception of a valuable service. But agents provide a very necessary and valuable service, and they are trained to look out for their clients' best interests. True salespeople are those who offer a valuable product or service—a product or service that they themselves also believe in.

Overcoming Emotional Hurdles

The real estate business can be very tough to endure emotionally. The reasons for that are not hard to find. You are trying to convince someone to do something that they, before now, decided not to do. You'll need to blanket many of your emotions while selling. More *bad* decisions are made based on emotion than logic. I'm going to go over what it takes to handle these human emotions in the best way in order to help you succeed.

Six Effective Ways to Handle Emotions

1. *Have confidence.* You must have confidence in your ability to succeed. If you have total confidence and believe in what you are selling, people can see past any handicaps that you may possess.

Confidence is so important in this business that if you don't have it, you will not thrive. People can easily spot weaknesses in others. That's what our primal instincts tell us to do. What I'm saying is that if you show that you are weak, you will be told what to do and not the other way around.

Remaining confident in the sales business is not so easy at first, especially if you don't know exactly what you are selling. Knowing and believing in what you offer is the best way to build your confidence wall. You must know, without a shadow of a doubt, that your product will benefit your client. If you honestly believe in what you are selling, you'll have no problem with remaining confident in your business. But in order to believe in what you sell, you must know all of the facts about your service—the pros, the cons, and everything in between. You need to know this so you can hold your head up and defend your service in face of objections by sellers. And you'll need to not only turn a bad situation around, but win them over.

2. *Battle intimidation.* In the beginning there was intimidation. This is the first psychological battle you must overcome in every new adventure you journey into. What is intimidation anyway? It's an emotion that triggers your lack of self-assurance when you're faced with a larger or "better" adversary. Maybe there's an agent in your office who you feel doesn't

like you, and you feel intimidated prospecting in front of him. Maybe you're afraid that you're going to make a mistake with a new client. Intimidation seems to always find its way into your actions. How do you get over this sensation?

The best way to get over intimidation is to break it down to see where it comes from. Hmm . . . where does intimidation come from? The fear of failure or the fear of *rejection*! You will probably face the rejection *with* intimidation. This is actually good. I know you're probably thinking to yourself, "How can that be good?" What I mean is, if you can face rejection early on in your career as much as possible, you will get accustomed to it and find it easier to accept. The best way to get over intimidation is to face it as much as possible. It will soon become old news and you'll find that there was no reason to be intimidated in the first place.

3. *Accept rejection.* Rejection is normal and it's everywhere. If you ever experienced rejection in this business, know this, the people aren't rejecting you, the people are rejecting the service you offer . . . *that's it.* But if you let rejection dig in too deep, it can slow you down physically and emotionally. It will also cut into your production. So here's what to do to combat rejection and get rid of it once and for all: Find out what each rejection is worth to you in dollars.

First you need to figure out how much your average commission is per sale. Divide that sale by how many phone calls it took to get that sale. That determines how much each call is worth for you. For example, let's say that your average commission per sale is $4,000, and you had to make 200 FSBO phone calls to get a listing that sold. That would imply that each call is worth $20. So when you call a FSBO and they tell you, "I'm not listing!" you can say, "I just made $20!" This is a good way to accept rejection and eliminate intimidation as well as some of the psychological stress that you face when calling FSBOs.

4. *Put off your anger.* One way of channeling your frustration and anger after a rejection is to deal with it at a later time. Tell yourself that you'll get mad about it in a week. Then when the time comes to let out your anger, you won't be angry any more. If you let your anger and frustration build up, your mood will show it and your clients will be uncomfortable with you. So next time someone tells you "Go shove it!" say to yourself, "I'll get mad about that in three days," and move on to the next call. Chances are, when the third day comes around, you'll be over your anger anyway.

5. *Don't give up.* Another critical ailment you must overcome is the urge to give up. *DON'T GIVE UP!* Sometimes I call hundreds of FSBOs in a

given week without listing a single one. This doesn't mean that I won't get four listings tomorrow or the next day. What that simply means is that the odds are in my favor of getting some listings very soon. People usually give up right before they are about to succeed. Think about it in this way. In a horse race, the winning horse often wins by only a nose. The winning horse gets the huge success of winning, although it took only the tip of the horse's nose to make it happen. When you push yourself to go an extra 10, 20, or 30 percent further than you are accustomed to, you can reap rewards in much greater percentages . . . I can guarantee that.

This may be the most important lesson in learning how to effectively prospect for FSBOs. Prospecting is purely a numbers game. The more prospects you call the better your odds are of getting listings, plain and simple. You *need* to apply this. Some new agents try calling a couple of FSBOs, encounter rejection, and call it quits. You can either let rejection get you down or you can defeat rejection. You must do the latter. I cannot stress this enough.

6. *Get motivated.* If you think that you can start off in real estate your first year and make a six-figure income without motivation, you're crazy. I won't delve into this topic, but please invest in some self-motivation CD's or books. I recom-

mend audio lessons by Tony Robbins and Tom Hopkins. Tony Robbins offers some highly motivational audio sessions to help you get into the mental attitude of becoming successful. Tom Hopkins is a master real estate sales expert, and his audio sessions relate directly to this industry. These are only two references, but there are many out there in book stores and online to choose from.

Self-Management

It's funny. I see many people working hard for their employers at a full- or part-time job, but when it comes to working for themselves, they won't give half the effort. When you think about it, you are your own business. You market yourself and sell yourself. Manage yourself like you would any other business. This requires you to do what it takes for you to run at your optimum efficiency. Treat your business like you treat yourself. Just do what's best for it.

Six Habits of Success

1. *Manage your time.* Let's look into how to make the numbers work for you. In order for you to get the most sales under your belt each year, you'll need to be efficient. This ultimately comes down to making business decisions on what the opportunity to prospect FSBOs is worth to you (also

called *opportunity cost,* in economic terms). In other words, know what your time is worth. If this is your first year, it's rather hard to know what your time is worth because you don't have an annual income number to punch into the equation. You can use your income goal for your first year. Be realistic. Divide the yearly income by twelve months, then divide that by thirty days, divide that by the number of hours you work per day and you'll figure out what you're worth per hour.

Let's do an example. Say your income goal for the year is to make $100,000 (after reading this book, of course).

- Divide $100,000 by 50 weeks (allowing 2 weeks for vacation).
- Divide $2,000 by 42 hours (5 days @ 8½ hrs).
- Your time is worth $47 per hour.

This hourly amount will help you decide whether something is worth your time or whether you can put that time to better use based on the money that you're worth per hour.

Let me give you a real-life example. If your time is worth $47 per hour, it wouldn't make much sense washing and ironing your dress clothes yourself, would it? Take them to the cleaners, save yourself two hours of work, and pay, say, only about $30 for that same work. By doing that you essentially just made yourself $64 by having someone else do your dirty work. I hope this makes sense to you.

Here's another example. Let's say that you are debating on whether to wash your car yourself by hand or go to a car wash. Well, if washing your car yourself would take an hour out of your work day, it is costing you $47 (using the hourly figure from above). If you were to bring your car to the car wash it would cost you $10. Well, I know which option is less costly, how about you? If you do the math you'll notice that washing your car will save you about $37. To keep things simple I did not factor in the time at the car wash, which is a variable.

This is the mentality that is necessary in order to be the most productive and efficient in working the numbers to your advantage. Now I don't expect people to over-analyze every decision in these terms, but these are just examples of how to use this in your everyday life. All of these little time- and money-saving decisions add up in the long run. You won't realize it in the short term because you can't actually see the money that you're implicitly saving, but when you look at your bank account at the end of the year it should be a pleasant surprise.

2. *Shake things up*. Organization is very important. When you get into a slump, which will happen once in a while, shake things up. Rearrange your

office, move around your office furniture, organize your files and paperwork, or tidy up your desk. In fact, when you do something "new" or "different," you change the pace at which you were comfortable, and in turn you procrastinate less. A change often helps you think of new ideas. Plus when you're organized it tends to make your work less complicated and helps you perform more efficiently. Organization can prevent disastrous listing presentations as well. The last thing you want to do is walk into a listing presentation with coffee rings on your listing agreement and dog-eared corners on your CMA (comparative market analysis).

3. *Schedule your tasks and appointments.* There are many organization ideas out there that help you with your daily tasks. One effective tool is a schedule software program for your computer. The program should have an option to set reminders for planned appointments and signal alerts to follow up with prospects in the future. You should print out your schedule every day and check off each task as you accomplish it. It feels good when you can see all that you've done each day in front of you on paper. This software program is also beneficial when it comes to calling FSBOs, as we'll see in Chapters 6 and 7. You can set alerts to remind you about follow-up calls that are due far off in the future. Otherwise

you might lose a Post-it Note to follow up with someone six months or a year from now. I highly recommend acquiring one of these software programs. You may also want to look into a PDA that offers scheduling software that is compatible with your computer.

4. *Don't procrastinate.* You can't do the same thing every day and expect different results. That old definition of *insanity* is still valid today for a good reason. Every real estate company has one or more agents that never set foot outside of the office. They talk on the phone most of the day, but never to potential prospects or clients; they also always have something negative to say about what the new agents are doing or how the market conditions are worsening. Their action is called procrastination. If you are one of these agents, *good!* Reading this book means, I hope, that you have recognized your problem and won't be one of these agents for long. But once you get into the bad habit of doing the same thing every day and expecting new results, it's hard to get out of that rhythm. If what you're doing is not working, then change what you're doing.

Procrastination is a disease that affects many of us. You sometimes don't know you have it until you recap what you've accomplished for the day. In order to prevent procrastination from taking control, you must change your pace. Don't let bad market news or office gossip affect you. Stay above it and focus on your success. Keep changing, keep learning, and keep challenging to take yourself to the next level of your career.

5. *Set goals.* Many people fail in life, not because they don't have what it takes to succeed, but because they lack a desirable goal. Goal setting should have a whole chapter devoted to it. Better yet, goal setting should have its own book. Having goals is probably the single most important factor that drives the wheel of success.

Establish your goals, and be realistic about them. Start a major goal with a timeline of ten years. Just think about where you want to be in ten years. Is it in a new home on the beach? How about being the top producer in the region? Whatever it may be, etch it in stone (not literally). Then establish a five-year goal, a one-year goal, a six-month goal, a one-month goal, a one-week goal, etc. Keep replenishing your short-term goals when they are fulfilled. Keep working toward your goals. Without goals you would have no reason to work to your highest potential and, ultimately, there would be no reason for you to be reading this book.

6. *Sharpen the saw.* In order for you to get from here to your goal you must overcome the many obstacles that will keep you from achieving your goals. The objective here is to try to eliminate as many

of those obstacles as possible first and foremost, before you work full force toward your goals. There is an old adage in the sales business, called *sharpen the saw.* Here is what it means. If you had to cut down a tree and all you had was a dull saw, would you start hacking at the tree with the dull saw or sharpen the saw first? The main reason for your sharpening the saw first is to pave the way for an efficient job and to maximize the results with the least amount of work overall. To put it in context for the real estate industry, sharpening the saw means being organized, prepared, and educated. You are essentially sharpening the saw by reading this book.

Taking Action

Create an action plan. What's an action plan without the action! Focus, hard work, determination, and goal setting—these are all parts of the plan. Incorporate them into your everyday life and take action.

Five Demands for Action

1. *Focus.* Think about a magnifying glass for a second. When you use it for examining small objects or fine print, it does the job just fine. But when you let the sun focus the magnifying glass into a tiny spec of light, it can create a *fire!* No gas, no spark, but simply focus makes the magnifying

glass become so powerful. This is important for you to realize. Focus on what you want in life. If your goal is to make six figures a year, or to be a top producer, you cannot do it without focus.

2. *Work hard.* I wasn't born to sell. I sculpted my skills and techniques in time by hard work and learning from my mistakes. It's hard work. Don't be mistaken. If you want to be successful in real estate you have to work at it. No one can enter the real estate profession and become successful without putting in the work. The will to work is based on how badly you want to become successful. If you want it, go get it. As Earl Nightingale says, "You are what you think about."

3. *Do it now!* There will always be work to do. The best motto for you to adopt is "DO IT NOW!" If you know you have something you have to do, don't put it off until later . . . DO IT NOW! Doing tasks right when you are faced with them will keep your work schedule lean and maximize your productivity. Not only should you DO IT NOW, but you should start your day with the task you fear and dread most. If you do what you fear and dread most first, it will harden your will to succeed and make the remaining tasks seem easy.

4. *Know your workload.* For every ten procrastinators you'll find one workaholic. Don't kill your-

self trying to get everything done at once. Your workload as a real estate agent is infinite. As long as you want to work in this business there will be work for you to do. That's one thing you don't have to worry about. Don't burn yourself out or start unhealthy habits because of your work schedule. That would be counterproductive. Balance your personal life with your business life with your family life. I suggest working fifty to sixty hours a week on your business and alloting the remaining 108 to 118 hours left in the week to family and personal life. Organize your weekly hours and designate time for family, friends, and recreation. Every person has a different lifestyle and family arrangement, so only you know what best fits you and your specific life to make it balanced.

5. *Take breaks.* When you start to feel like you're burning out, take a break. Each workday you should have at least three breaks. This is important because you need to unwind, gain steam, and jump back in the game without burning out. When you burn out you become bitter, your attitude changes from upbeat to grumpy, and this undermines your mission. Burning out is also bad for your health. Too much stress increases your blood pressure and leads to a myriad of illnesses. So for yourself, and for your surrounding environment (including your clients and prospects),

take as many breaks as you need in order to always to be at your best.

Living Healthy

A healthy lifestyle is just as important as your career is to you. It is very important that you keep your body and mind in good shape. This business can easily exhaust you physically and mentally. Be good to your body and it will be good to you.

Seven Tips for a Healthy Business Life

1. *Exercise.* Working out and exercising on a regular basis will keep you at your best. Exercise keeps your sales skills sharp and nourishes your physical and mental health. When you work out in the morning, your body's metabolism remains high throughout the day. This will keep you energized and ready to take on the day. Also, joining a gym can have other benefits, such as meeting new people and being able to prospect for new clients.

2. *Eat smart.* I know there are times when you are too busy to prepare a lean, healthy meal, so you swing through a drive-through and buy the most fatty sandwich and chase it down with a soda and fries. This acts like sand in an engine. You're only slowing yourself down by doing this. Your body uses more energy breaking down chemically processed, high saturated-fat foods than lean,

healthy foods. This ultimately leaves less energy for you. A good, fast alternative could be a neighborhood deli, or something on the menu that can't be bad for you, such as a salad. Look at other alternatives as well. Perhaps try making yourself a lunch. Making a lunch can save you time, money, and doesn't slow you down like fast food.

3. *Eat often.* Eat when you're hungry. Don't put off eating and go starving while making phone calls. Hunger will distract you while you work. How can you focus on selling yourself and your services and think about food at the same time? You won't perform at your best if you do. Furthermore, eating *too* much will do quite the opposite. People oftentimes eat when they procrastinate. This leads to an unhealthy lifestyle. Try to find your balance. What I find to work best is to take many small breaks and eat modest portions. Such a routine will prevent you from being "stuffed" and also gives you the breaks you need to keep sane and not burn out.

4. *Don't smoke.* More and more these days the sophisticated public is becoming aware of the repercussions of smoking. It's going out of style fast. If you're a smoker and refuse to quit, that's fine, but it will cost you thousands of dollars every year in unsuccessful listing appointments, not to mention the cost of the cigarettes that seem to have no

price ceiling. It's a hefty price to pay, no matter which way you look at it. Think of it this way: If you don't care about your own health, how can you convince your potential clients that you care for them and their needs? It's a tough sell.

5. *Sleep.* Everyone loves their sleep. As a FSBO specialist, you need every minute of it. There are two things in selling that will never go together, drowsiness and staying sharp. The phone is your main tool, and in order to stay sharp and keep focused, you need to have the energy that only sleep can give you. By the same token, too much sleep could have adverse effects. A reasonable time frame would be between seven and nine hours. Aim for just enough to stay sharp but not too much to put you into a comatose slump.

6. *Start early.* Start your day early and go to bed early. Just think about how you can maximize your work hours. When you wake up early, your business day is longer and you get more work done before the end of the day. If you wake up early, naturally, you should get tired early. The idea is to get into this routine so that you don't find it hard to wake up early in the morning.

Waking up early will also give you a competitive advantage against other agents. Because we agents are technically self-employed, most of us tend to wake up when we feel like it. Prospecting

FSBOs before other agents do will keep you ahead of the game and maximize your listing potential.

7. *Think energy.* Think energy, don't drink energy. It's not good walking into a listing appointment with the impression that you're on *speed*. If your mouth is talking 200 miles per hour you'll only scare your sellers, which won't help you close on a listing. Try not to abuse caffeine. Drinking coffee is one thing but don't start pumping your heart with high doses of caffeine to make it work harder just because *you* don't want to work hard.

CHAPTER 3

FSBO Prospecting Plan

Men who are resolved to find a way for themselves will always find opportunities enough; and if they do not find them, they will make them.

—SAMUEL SMILES

FSBO Fact

Ninety percent of homebuyers used a real estate agent in their search for a home, while 77 percent of homebuyers purchased their home through a real estate agent or broker, according to the NAR study.

SOURCE: National Association of Realtors®,
Profile of Home Buyers and Sellers, 2005.

Seeing a For-Sale-By-Owner yard sign should evoke the same feelings you would get from seeing a blank check with your name on it. The potential with FSBOs is endless. And the good part is that FSBOs will always be there for you. In good times or bad times, guess what . . . there will be FSBOs.

Here are some topics discussed in this chapter:

- Defining your FSBO boundaries
- How to find FSBOs
- Where to find FSBOs
- Using the Internet for leads
- Bringing FSBOs to you
- Using Open Houses to find FSBOs

Defining Your FSBO Boundaries

Once in a while you'll come across a FSBO in a newspaper classified ad and you'll ask yourself, "Do I really want to work that far away?" Before you start collecting FSBO ads to build your database, you'll need to define your territory. That way, when you find a good source of FSBO leads you'll know which ones to take and which ones to pass up. I will personally trek up to a twenty-mile radius from my office for a listing. I feel that it's worth it for me to stay within those boundaries. You must determine yours. If you only concentrate on listings in a small neighborhood, you'll limit yourself and your income. Try to take them where they come, within reason.

How to Find FSBOs

If you're just getting started prospecting for FSBOs you'll need to look in a variety of places. Start with the

FSBOs that you already have, but eventually you'll need a list of at least 200 to 300 FSBOs to effectively make the numbers work to your advantage. Over time, your list should grow to the point where you can call FSBOs five days a week and not run out of FSBOs to call. If you're struggling on ways to find FSBOs, first you'll have to think like a FSBO.

Newspaper Classified Ads

One of the first advertising media FSBOs turn to is the newspaper classifieds. This will probably be your main source of FSBO leads. In many cities there are several newspapers with classified sections. Try to get your hands on as many as you can. Keep this in mind, the best FSBO leads are the ones that not many other agents know about.

How to Spot a FSBO

Sometimes it's difficult to spot which newspaper ads are FSBOs and which are listed with an agent in the classified section. It seems that all of the ads run together and are hard to distinguish from one another. So here's a tip. In most states, by law, if a property is listed through a licensed real estate agent, the advertisement must indicate just that. For most ads you should be able to tell whether they are listed or not. Sometimes the only thing that distinguishes the listed ads from the FSBOs is a small code, usually on the bottom of the ad, which the office uses to reference which property that ad belongs to. And almost always, a real estate office will not list the address of the property in the ad, a tactic used to entice buyers to call in to get the address and speak with an agent.

However, be careful. Agents who do their own advertising and who may be unaware of the advertising laws may not indicate that the property is listed. I can remember calling many supposed "FSBOs" and finding an agent on the other end of the line. What I will often do is inform the agent that they are breaking the law and jeopardizing their license. And, of course, they'll act like they didn't know about that law.

FSBO Magazines

There are magazines out there that specialize in advertising FSBOs. These are a great resource for FSBO leads. The reason these are so good is because not many agents find or use them. You can find these magazines in many large stores' entry- and exit-ways. You can also get free subscriptions to some of these magazines through many of the FSBO websites.

Public Ads

You can pretty much find FSBOs where you find any other advertising. You may see ads taped onto light poles near busy traffic intersections. Many grocery stores have a tack board for a lost dog or a car for sale or a FSBO! You should be able to find these public-style advertisements in convenient stores, restaurants, gas stations, or video rental stores. Just about any place where you'll find an entry or exit foyer with free magazines, you'll have a chance of finding homemade FSBO ads. These are often the best

FSBO ads. Many times, these will be the only ads the seller will post, which will ensure that you won't have much competition, and that they haven't had and won't get much activity.

FSBO Lead-Providers

If you're already a licensed real estate agent, you may have received e-mails from some services that provide FSBO leads in your area. For a monthly fee you can usually get a great number of leads from these providers, daily or weekly. Most of these services get their leads from some of the same sources from which you would get yours. This is a great way to give a boost to your FSBO database, not to mention that this is also a great time saver. Keep in mind, though, they won't have every FSBO that is out there. You can still find the "prime" FSBOs, which are the ones that most other agents don't know about and which therefore have less competition. I delve into FSBO lead provider services in Chapter 5.

Where to Find FSBOs

There are many FSBOs that don't advertise in newspapers nor make flyers. These types of FSBOs are harder to find but are worth much more because you won't have as much competition with them. The only way to find this type of FSBO is to do it the hard way. You're going to have to drive around and comb neighborhoods block by block. After a while, it starts to become fun. It's like finding the hidden Easter eggs.

Farm FSBOs

You should drive by your local farm area every week and look for new FSBOs (also to scope out your competition). And when you do so, make sure you have your car magnet advertisements on (we'll get into that later). When you find a FSBO yard sign, take down the phone number and note as much information about the house as possible, such as the style, exterior type, condition, etc. When you pull up to a FSBO, after you've written down the phone number, go up and ring their doorbell. Introduce yourself to them as the neighborhood real estate agent and also give them a FSBO Package, which we'll discuss next.

FSBO Package

A FSBO Package is a concise bundle of marketing information that is specifically geared toward FSBOs. Your FSBO Package should include your resume, FSBO statistics information (samples of both are shown in the Appendix), and your business card, all in a neat folder.

When the seller answers the doorbell, you can say something like this:

"Hi, I'm [Your Name] with [Your Company] Realty. I noticed that you're selling by owner and just wanted to drop off my information in case you choose a different route in the future, is that okay with you?"

And when you call the FSBO later, you can say:

"Hi, this is [Your Name] with [Your Company] Realty. I introduced myself to you the other day and gave you my information . . . *remember me?*"

This will burn your name into their brain, and they'll remember you until it's time to list.

If the seller is not home, leave the FSBO Package at their door, and make a note of it. This way, when you call them you'll have something to mention:

"Hi, this is [Your Name] with [Your Company] Realty. I saw that your home is for sale by owner. Did you get the information that I left for you?"

When you call FSBOs who already have your information, there's a great likelihood that they'll listen to what you have to say.

For Rent by Owners

Although these properties are not for sale, For Rent signs can be a good source of leads. When a seller or landlord is trying to rent out an apartment, this usually means that they aren't getting a rental income, at least not for the unit that is for rent. This may be a seller who is desperate to sell or who may be sick of being a landlord. Take down the information from For Rent signs as you come across them. You'll be surprised how many of these will end up as viable leads.

Clean-Out Businesses

Clean-out businesses, if you're not familiar with them, are companies that are hired by a seller to clean out their home. They either clean out all trash left behind, or they buy and remove the contents of an estate. The bottom line is that they deal mostly with estate sales. Many if not most estate sales are handled by someone who inherits the property and has no clue of what to do with it. That is where you come in handy.

Contact as many of these clean-out businesses as you can. Mail them your card and ask for some of their cards. Convince them that you'll be giving their cards out to people who are moving and need the services of a clean-out business (it happens). In turn, ask them to give your card out to all of their customers.

Estate sales are often some of the best listings you will get. They sell quickly because the majority of them are outdated and need some work, and they get priced accordingly. When you get an estate sale listing, ask the sellers for permission to put "Estate Sale" in the remarks of the listing sheet. This will bring in many more people who perceive estate sales as an opportunity for a bargain.

Using the Internet to Find FSBOs

Another good medium for locating FSBOs is the Internet. Your local newspapers should have an online edition, and you'll notice that many FSBOs only advertise online. Just look up your local newspaper's website and find their classified section. You can search the classified section online just as easy as, if not easier than, the print edition. Don't just end it there. There are many more areas to explore for FSBOs online than you may have thought.

Go exploring for yourself. You'll find many websites that host FSBOs. Just be sure to read the fine print. On some of these websites, they prohibit the solicitation of real estate agents. You can look under "Homes for Sale" on websites like craigslist.com and buyowner.com. Many by-owner sites offer FSBO leads as well. Like I said earlier, FSBOs are everywhere. *Why aren't you calling them?*

Bringing FSBOs to You

To be the most efficient, and essentially to make the most money, you must delegate. Having people calling you with FSBO information is another way to gather leads. You can try paying a couple of bucks for every unique FSBO the mailperson, the paperboy, or friends and family give you.

It's also a very good idea to delegate someone to find and clip out FSBO classified ads and input them into your FSBO database. Remember opportunity cost. Figure out how long it would take you to do this chore yourself and see if it's worth it for you to hire someone else to do it instead.

Another way to bring FSBOs to you is to entice them to call *you*. How do you do that? Well, you have to convince them that you know more about selling their home than they do. Send them all of the overwhelming paperwork that they'll need for their transaction as well as information about staging the home and holding open houses. This is what I call the FSBO S.O.S. Package:

FSBO S.O.S. Package

- Sample offer contract
- Local HUD disclosures
- Sample mortgage approval letter
- Sample inspection report
- Open house tips
- Home improvement tips
- Your resume
- FSBO statistics (proving that FSBOs net less than listed homes)

When they see the vast knowledge you have about selling a home, they'll be impressed and call you when they realize they need an agent.

Using Open Houses to Find FSBOs

Holding an open house offers the opportunity for a great source of leads from buyers and, more importantly, from neighbors who are thinking of selling. While it's rare (in most markets) to sell the house you're holding open, you set a stage that attracts new prospects to you. And for only three or four hours out of your day, you should always be up for this task.

Five Tips for Staging an Open House

1. *Brighten it up.* Turn on the lights in ⌐ are dim (without overkill). Making a home ιυ bright can show imperfections and take away from a relaxed mood. If it's a sunny day, open the shades and show off the natural light the home gets.

2. *Rid all odors.* If there are funky smells going on in your open house, try your best to get rid of them. You can light candles, buy some pleasant scented flowers, or bake some cookies. The smell of baked goods will give buyers a natural homey feel while they walk through the property. For animal smells there are special odor removers that you can purchase.

3. *Turn on the tunes.* Bring a radio to your open house and play some easy listening music. This should make buyers more comfortable in the home and give them a soundtrack to remember the home by when they leave. This also avoids awkward silences.

4. *Clean it up.* Don't hold an open house if the home is a wreck; you'll only make yourself look bad. Kindly ask the sellers to clean up before the open. I know this is hard to do with some sellers. You can try saying something like: "Mr. Seller, having a shipshape home is important when attracting

buyers. Will the home be tidy for the open house?"

5. *Turn the home on.* If the home has features such as a fireplace, central air conditioning, or a backyard pond, then turn them on. Show that the home is fully functional and you'll make it more welcoming. Of course, you wouldn't turn on the air conditioning in the winter, nor the fireplace in the summer. On extremely hot summer days, crank up the A/C so they get hit with a cool breeze at the front door. They'll never want to leave!

Your open house should be free of sellers. Ask your sellers to leave during the open house by saying, "You *will* be leaving during the open house, *won't you?*" If they say no, then explain to them why it is important that they do.

Reasons the Sellers Should Not Attend

- Buyers need to get emotionally involved with the property without the sellers present.
- The agent can sell the home better than the homeowners can.
- Buyers like to take their time and not feel under pressure.
- Removing the seller prevents the buyer from talking directly with the seller.
- The buyer will not be able to "read" the seller and feel out their motivations for selling.

The Neighbors

Your first open house on a listing is oftentimes your best. Keep this in mind also: The first open house will bring more neighbors than any subsequent ones. Neighbors that visit your open house are doing it for one primary reason: They want to know how much their home is worth by comparison. They may be thinking of selling by owner and are conducting their own market analysis, or they may just be curious which homes are selling in their neighborhood.

If your intentions for holding an open house are to sell the listing, you're in for a surprise. Unless you are in an extremely hot housing market, this rarely happens. If you're trying to get buyer leads, you'll need an open house that is priced at market value and in a high traffic location to get potential buyers in the door. But if your aim is to get more listings, you'll need to accomplish a bit more.

At your first open house you'll find that many of the guests that sign in are living in the immediate area. This means that they are probably homeowners, and not buyers for the property. Once you find this out ask them questions along that tangent, such as:

- Are you currently working with an agent?
- How long have you lived in this neighborhood?
- When are you thinking of making a move?
- Where are you thinking of moving to?
- Do you know the current value of your home?

After you question them and find their motivations, try to close for an appointment. Offer them a free CMA and give them your resume and business card. Tell them that having a listing in the area gives you an upper hand in selling other properties in the neighborhood because you'll get more buyers that call on your signs.

The day after you hold an open house, mail the open-house neighbor prospects a thank you letter (hand-written) and a list of all of the homes you and your office have recently sold in the area. This should get you into their door. If you don't close for the appointment, follow up periodically until you do.

CHAPTER 4

Know Thy Competition

My philosophy of life is that if we make up our mind what we are going to make of our lives, then work hard toward that goal, we never lose—somehow we win out.

—RONALD REAGAN

FSBO Fact

Thirty-two percent of people who bought directly from sellers knew them in advance of the transaction, meaning that about one-third of **FSBO** transactions are not placed on the open market.

SOURCE: National Association of Realtors®, *Profile of Home Buyers & Sellers, 2005.*

In this chapter I'm going to break down your competition and how to remain competitive. Competition can be intimidating at times, but it is important to look at it in this way. It forces you to become the best you can be. Without competition you wouldn't have the need to have goals, which challenge yourself and shape your character. You must also remember, there will always be room in this industry for one more top producer.

Defeating your competition takes strategy and skill. If there is any one area in the real estate industry where you'll find competition, it is with FSBOs. Because FSBOs are the most abundant leads, agents and marketing companies are going to compete with each other to get them. There are three fundamental components that stand out from the array of competition you will face while working with FSBOs. These are:

1. FSBO websites and publications
2. Discount brokerages
3. Other agents

FSBO Websites

There are websites out there that offer FSBOs limited Internet advertisement and some paper advertisement. Most of these sites charge a hefty up-front fee that is nonrefundable, even if the home doesn't sell. The cost of advertising with these sites can range from $1,000 to well over $6,000, and most don't even get you on the MLS (multiple listing service), which, as you probably know, is the single most important advertising medium . . . *period!*

Here is an important statistic that will aid you in winning over the competition. In 2006, 84 percent of all home sales involved using an agent, according to the National Association of Realtors®. Why is that? Well, agents have a slew of tools at their fingertips, including the MLS. Agents have the negotiation experience and know how to handle all of the paperwork and legal ramifications involved in a transaction. Furthermore, homes advertised through these website services get listed with agents eventually anyway. That means that the FSBOs' initial ad money gets wasted.

First and foremost, your goal should be to convince FSBOs to not waste their time and money with these advertisement mediums. When you use this approach make sure you know which websites are popular in your area as well as the pros and cons of each.

The Seven Disadvantages of Most FSBO Websites:

1. They do NOT list the property on the MLS!!!
2. They have very limited Internet advertising.
3. The FSBO has to do all of the leg work, showings, and open houses.
4. There is a hefty up-front fee that is nonrefundable, *even if the home doesn't sell.*
5. There is no professional from whom to seek advice, or with whom to go over the paperwork and legal documents.
6. There is no experienced negotiator to get the best price for the home.
7. FSBOs don't have the tools to do an accurate

CMA. This typically leads to overpriced listings that don't sell.

Discount Brokers

A discount broker is a licensed real estate brokerage company that is set up a little differently from the typical brokerage firm. If you're not familiar with discount brokers, here's how they work. Discount brokers are just like the typical brokerage firm except they lack the most fundamental ingredient: *a sales agent!* The discount broker, then, stays out of the picture and hands all duties and responsibilities to the seller. When sellers want to list their homes on the MLS with a real estate agent and avoid paying the full brokerage fee, they list with a discount brokerage. Discount brokers usually charge a flat fee for processing the listing on the MLS—something in the range of $250 to $1,000—and the seller just pays the co-op agent, that is, the agent who brings in the buyer. The seller assumes the responsibility to do all other advertising, showings, open houses, and negotiating.

The Seven Disadvantages of Most Discount Brokers

1. The seller pays more than half the average brokerage fee for less than half of the marketing services of a full-service broker.
2. Agents who have a buyer for a property listed with a discount broker usually don't feel comfortable negotiating offers directly with the seller.

3. The seller will have no professional to guide them through the transaction to closing.
4. There is no experienced agent to negotiate offers.
5. The seller has to do all of the legwork, additional advertising, showings, and manage all open houses.
6. The listing discount brokerage firm usually will not hold the buyer's earnest money check.
7. With no incentive for the discount brokerage firm to sell the property, they'll make no extra effort to do so.

Other Agents

Every real estate agent is aware that FSBOs are open leads that anyone can compete for. But most agents are not FSBO specialists. As I stated earlier, only 5 percent of agents focus on prospecting them. Don't get me wrong, many FSBOs do get contacted by agents. Most of these agents will call them once, and then never again. This is where you will have to fill a gap. A FSBO specialist like yourself will be able to win over the competition by using the proven techniques in this book that most other agents aren't even aware of.

The advantages you'll have over most agents are the tools and marketing statistics that will benefit FSBOs directly. With that being said, you will appeal to FSBOs as a problem solver who suits their specific needs and who understands them on their level.

The Seven Disadvantages of Most "Other" Agents

1. About 95 percent of agents do not prospect FSBOs and therefore don't understand their needs.
2. Most agents give up on a FSBO after the first call.
3. Most agents will take a FSBO listing overpriced.
4. Many agents work only part time, not giving their listings the attention they deserve.
5. About 86 percent of new agents don't make it past their first year . . . *but not you!*
6. Working with FSBOs requires you to be aggressive, which is a trait that is scarcely found among agents.
7. A great percentage of agents won't read a book in order to further their career. Your reading this book is, in and of itself, an accomplishment that will benefit your clients.

Preparing Yourself for the Competition

In order for you to stay ahead of your competition you'll have to get to know them. Whether it's other offices or other agents, discount brokers, or FSBO marketing services, you'll need to weigh what they offer against what you offer and compare it pound for pound.

You vs. the Competition

Create a tally chart. In the first column list yourself, and then list all of your competitors below your name. Add a column for each marketing medium you offer, and then put a check next to the competitors that can match that offer. A sample tally chart is shown in Figure 4-1.

	MLS	Local Paper	Specialty Paper	Custom Sign	Web Ads	CMA
You	☑	☑	☑	☑	☑	☑
Other Agent	☑	☑		☑		☑
Other Office	☑	☑			☑	☑
Discount Broker	☑					
FSBO Website			☑		☑	

Figure 4-1. Sample tally sheet of the marketing mediums offered compared to the competition.

Being Aggressive

There are several books aimed at helping FSBOs to succeed going it alone. I suggest brushing up on some of those books to get an idea of what FSBOs are reading and looking for. What I found is that some of these books even suggest listing with an agent if selling by owner is not successful. They go even further to mention that FSBOs should look for an aggressive agent.

Here is the textbook definition of *aggressive: Making an all-out effort to win or succeed.* An aggressive sales approach would characterize someone who exhausts all options in order to achieve their aim. You must leave no stone unturned in order to convince someone that you are an aggressive agent. FSBOs want you to take charge and not have to worry about the details. This requires them to put their trust in you. And you must prove to them that you are worthy of it.

Offering Full Service

Many FSBOs choose to go a different route simply because they can't handle the transaction without the help of a professional. Offering "full service" can relieve your clients of the worry and stress involved in maintaining the sale of their home. Full service can mean something different to every agent. My definition of full service is *someone who is willing to do whatever it takes to effectively market and sell a property while keeping the seller updated every step of the way.*

This may entail personally conducting all of the showings for your listings yourself, personally doing open houses every Sunday, and giving your seller an update on the activity and neighborhood market twice a week. The idea behind offering "full service" is to get your seller to put their trust in you to take control of the transaction. More on servicing your listing in Chapter 12.

CHAPTER 5

The FSBO System

Champions keep playing until they get it right.

—BILLIE JEAN KING

FSBO Fact

FSBOs have no access to fundamental marketing services, such as the Multiple Listing Service (MLS), and they cannot list their homes there. They also have no access to other marketing avenues such as REALTOR.com, Virtual Office websites, and the Internet Data Exchange.

SOURCE: National Association of Realtors®,
Profile of Home Buyers & Sellers, 2005.

In this chapter you'll learn how to implement systems into place that will drastically improve your means to prospect FSBOs. This is a very important chapter of this book because without a system, there is no direction.

The Tools

One very important aspect of prospecting is to be able to do it as efficiently as possible. That's why I created the FSBO System. Now I'm going to introduce two tools to you:

1. FSBO Number Check

2. FSBO Journal

These two tools are essential for keeping track of the FSBOs that you call on a daily basis and for helping you stay on top of your business. You'll need Microsoft Excel or a similar program to lay out the template for both the FSBO Number Check and for the FSBO Journal. You'll also need a little patience at first if you're not familiar with Excel.

First, I want to inform you about why I created these programs. Probably one of the most humiliating things you can do is call a FSBO twice without realizing it. Some FSBOs may run two different ads or change the language in the advertisement article and throw you off. So I came up with a very simple number check to prevent you from calling the same FSBO twice, permanently.

FSBO Number Check

The following seven steps show you how to create the FSBO Number Check. You'll need Excel; if you don't have it, use your office's computer or just purchase the Excel program.

1. Open a new Microsoft Excel document.
2. In column 1, row 1, type in your first FSBO phone number in the box. Input the ten-digit phone number without spaces or hyphens, and don't put a 1 in front of the area code.

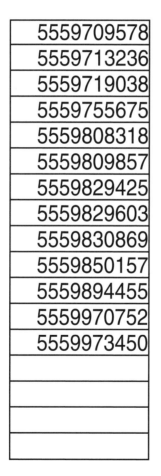

5559709578
5559713236
5559719038
5559755675
5559808318
5559809857
5559829425
5559829603
5559830869
5559850157
5559894455
5559970752
5559973450

Figure 5-1. FSBO Number Check: Sorted telephone numbers.

3. Continue to input your FSBO numbers down the first column only until you have listed them all. Your list should look something like Figure 5-1.

5559669510
5559677852
5559679861
5559700829
5559708442
5559709578
5559713236
5559719038
5559755675
5559808318
5559809857
5559829425
5559829603
5558789269
5558905540
5558958448
5558993464
5559103729

Figure 5-2. FSBO Number Check: Adding new numbers in bold.

Highlight the entire column of numbers and put them in ascending numerical order by clicking the "Sort Ascending" button, which looks like this: (This button puts things in alphabetical *and* numerical order.)

4. Then, as you get *new* FSBO phone numbers to check against your existing numbers, input them below the existing list. Make them bold. This will distinguish them from the originals, as shown in Figure 5-2.

5. Highlight the whole column again and put them in numerical order by clicking the "Sort Ascending" button again.

6. Scroll through and check to see if the bold numbers have a double above or below it. If you have a double, delete it from the list (see Figure 5-3).

7. When you've deleted the duplicates, put all of the remaining numbers into regular font so the chart is ready for the next time you run the number check. Of course, make sure you save the file after each use to update your new list.

If you update your phone list on a regular basis, there's now no reason for you to be worried about accidentally calling a FSBO twice. This also saves a lot of time since you no longer need to comb through all of your newspaper clippings checking for doubles.

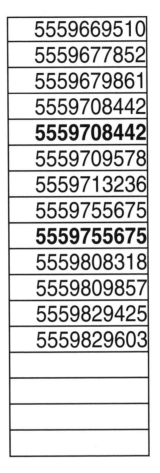

5559669510
5559677852
5559679861
5559708442
5559708442
5559709578
5559713236
5559755675
5559755675
5559808318
5559809857
5559829425
5559829603

Figure 5-3. FSBO Number Check: Deleting the duplicates.

The FSBO Journal

Now we come to the second part of your FSBO toolkit, and the most important part: the FSBO Journal. This is a template that organizes your FSBO information in an orderly, efficient arrangement, which allows you to log specific details about every FSBO phone call you make. You can record conversation topics, home features, and name of seller or sellers; gauge FSBOs as to their potential for listing; and note precisely when to call them back. This way you'll always be prepared when you make that second, third, or tenth call down the line.

How to Create the FSBO Journal

1. Open a new Microsoft Excel document.

Phone: 555-736-2984	Name: Jason Smith	Call Back: 4/15
Address: 123 Addison	Remarks: Nice guy	4/28 5/10
Area: Chicago - Portage Park	Married w/2 kids	
Bed/Bath: 3br/2bth	Prop. Type: Brick bungalow	Potential: Hot !!
Ask: $350,000	Cond: Recent remodel	Class: A

Phone:	Name:	Call Back:
Address:	Remarks:	
Area:		
Bed/Bath:	Prop. Type:	Potential:
Ask:	Cond:	Class:

Phone:	Name:	Call Back:
Address:	Remarks:	
Area:		
Bed/Bath:	Prop. Type:	Potential:
Ask:	Cond:	Class:

Phone:	Name:	Call Back:
Address:	Remarks:	
Area:		
Bed/Bath:	Prop. Type:	Potential:
Ask:	Cond:	Class:

Phone:	Name:	Call Back:
Address:	Remarks:	
Area:		
Bed/Bath:	Prop. Type:	Potential:
Ask:	Cond:	Class:

Phone:	Name:	Call Back:
Address:	Remarks:	
Area:		
Bed/Bath:	Prop. Type:	Potential:
Ask:	Cond:	Class:

Figure 5-4. FSBO Journal.

2. Organize the cells as shown in Figure 5-4. Fit five templates on a page.

3. Save the file and print out one copy to use for making additional copies. Then organize these templates on a traditional clipboard or 3-ring binder.

How to Use the FSBO Journal Template

You can organize the cells of the FSBO Journal template to your specific liking. Before calling your FSBOs, run new phone numbers against the numbers on your FSBO Number Check. Then input numbers that are unique into your FSBO Journal. Fill in the templates as best you can with the information given on the newspaper ad, signs, or other sources. When you start calling your FSBOs, use the templates to guide you through some of the questioning. If there are any blank fields, use these as a basis for asking the sellers questions, and then fill in as much important information as they will give you over the phone. Include memorable conversation topics in the "Remarks" section so you can bring them up when you make your next calls. That way, they will easily remember who you are. Always record a call-back date so you'll know whether you're calling them on time or if it's still too soon. Right after speaking with sellers, mark their potential to list. You can cross off the ones that have either sold or have already listed with an agent. But *DO NOT* cross off *anyone* who says they don't want to work with an agent. *You must keep calling everyone until they list, sell, or die* . . . no exceptions to the rule! You may have to keep calling some

FSBOs for over a year before they list, but on the other hand there will be some sellers who list on the first call.

If you are not a good phone person, then you'll have to learn how to be one. In Chapters 6 and 7, we'll dive into the basics for handling the phone. I recommend investing in a how-to book for phone sales. Investments like these give great returns. With time you can gain the experience to know what to expect and be prepared for every type of phone conversation. But it takes time, drilling, and rehearsal. You can't become a pro in one day. You must be patient and persistent.

Ranking the FSBO by Personality

When you record your FSBO information into your templates, you'll want to have as much information at your fingertips as possible. One great way to be prepared for a follow-up call is to know what type of seller you're calling back.

FSBOs can be categorized into four personality classes, from Class A to Class D. When first talking to a FSBO, characterize their personality according to one of these four classes and then record that class on your template in preparation for the next call. That way you'll be ready for each personality class before you call.

Four Personality Classes of a FSBO

- The **Class A** personalities are the sellers who are going FSBO because they don't know any better.

They are usually friendly and willing to put their trust in others. These personalities take compliments well. These FSBOs will consider listing very soon. Oftentimes these are first-time sellers.

- **Class B** FSBOs are the intellectual, open-minded types. They think that they will make money by selling it themselves, but they will listen to what you have to say and consider it. They want bottom-line information to make an educated decision on whether to list with you or go a different route.

- **Class C** sellers are the talkative ones. You can let these sellers talk until they reveal their motivations. They especially love talking about themselves and their home. These sellers are going FSBO because they "heard" it's easy to do and that it saves them from paying a commission. It is your job to convince them otherwise.

- **Class D** sellers may have had a bad experience with an agent in the past, may think they can do a better job than an agent, or just don't want to spend the money. Many are rude at first, but they can be won over. They usually have a lot of pride in self-accomplishment. These are tough sells but are still list-able. *DO NOT GIVE UP ON THESE!*

Class B and C personalities are ones that you'll encounter most. It is important that you do your best in determining which personality class a FSBO falls into and mark it in your FSBO Journal. Also, don't give up on Class D sellers. The reason for this is because every other real estate agent already has given up on them. Therefore, you'll have very little competition with this type of seller. When they decide to list, you'll be first in line.

If You're an Excel Pro

If you have experience in using Microsoft Excel, you can be even more effective using your FSBO Journal. Use your computer to type in your FSBO information, remarks, call-back dates, etc. More importantly you can insert pictures of each FSBO and color-code their level of potential to list. This should make it easier for you to comb through and find the ones with the highest potential to call first. I call this more sophisticated FSBO Journal the "Journal Pro," an example of which is shown in Figure 5-5.

	Phone: 555-2592	Call Back: **7/28**	Remarks: Interested in listing
	Address: 555 NEWLAND	Name: Mr. Murphy	Saw the inside... has partially
		AskP: $279,900	finished basement. Very nice
	Br's/Bth's: 2/1	Market date: 6/1	people.
	Hot	Condition:	
	Area: Portage Park	Style: Bungalow	Class: A

	Phone: 555-6665	Call Back: **7/30**	Remarks: Home is under
	Address:123 Oak Park	Name: Jeff Smith	contract. Follow up!
		AskP: $386,000	
	Br's/Bth's: 3/2	Market date:	
	Under Contract	Condition:	
	Area: Montclare	Style: English Tudor	Class: C

Figure 5-5. Journal Pro.

Take Pictures

Taking pictures will give you a reason to visit each and every FSBO in your database. Ring the doorbell of the

FSBO and introduce yourself in person. And if they're not home, leave your FSBO Package. Take a picture of the property with your digital camera and insert the picture into your template, as shown in Figure 5-5.

Color-Code Your Potential

Instead of writing in the words that describe how much potential the lead has, just color-code it on your computer. This makes it easier to sift through. You can scroll through your Journal Pro to find the "hot" ones.

Make Use of Your Photos

Since you'll already have a picture of the FSBOs that you're prospecting, make use of them in other ways. You can create a professional brochure for FSBOs, showing a picture of their home. Make sure you make these brochures better than anything that they can make them-selves, so that they'll use yours over theirs. On the top corner of the page put that this home is for sale by owner. However, on the opposite corner add this sentence: "This brochure was created courtesy of (Your Name) with (Your Company) Realty," and put your contact information underneath. Now when buyers grab these brochures, they'll call you for information.

This brochure will give you a great reason to call the seller. Not only that, but it's an excellent show of aggressiveness from the seller's point of view. And if they were to hire anyone, they'll hire someone who is already doing a great job for them, wouldn't you agree?

Subscribing to FSBO Lead Provider Services

There are several FSBO lead provider services out there. What a FSBO lead provider does is sift through all of your local newspaper and Internet classified sections for FSBO ads. They compile them on a daily or weekly basis and send them to you through an e-mail. This can be a great time saver for you. Not only do they usually generate an abundance of leads, but the leads are from a variety of sources, which gives you some leverage against other competing agents. (For some FSBO lead provider referrals, see the resources in the Appendix.)

Is It Worth It?

You bet! The monthly investment for this type of service will range from $20 to about $80 per month at the time of this writing. The opportunity cost of this type of investment will reap you major returns. It saves you a tremendous amount of time. Better yet, convince your broker to pick up the tab. Just say that this will increase the office's listing inventory and ultimately lead to more sales. If you don't want to share this great secret with the other agents in your office, just include it in your monthly budget. But remember, only about 5 percent of agents prospect FSBOs. That would mean if you had 100 agents in your office, only about five would be sharing this information with you. That's not so bad.

FSBO Leads Are Safe!

A great feature of these lead provider services is that they check their phone numbers against the Do Not Call List. You can feel safe dialing a FSBO number now that you know that there's no possibility of getting slammed with a fine.

They also check numbers against doubles. So, if you decide to join one of these services, you won't need to use your FSBO Number Check after all. The FSBO lead provider will do all of the number-checking work for you. This should take a load of work off your shoulders and help ease your mind about calling unique leads.

E-Mail FSBO Leads

Some of the FSBO lead provider services will e-mail you leads along with the seller's e-mail address. This is a great resource that is rare to come by. Especially for new agents who may just be getting over the fear of the phone, these e-mail leads are gold.

Make a personal advertisement to e-mail the FSBO seller. Be sure to customize the e-mail with FSBO statistics and disadvantages about selling by owner (see Appendix B), and demonstrate your knowledge of the market in which their home is for sale. Take your time. You are not under pressure with these leads. Include a concise resume in this e-mail along with your recent achievements or sales. If they don't e-mail or call you back, send a follow up e-mail. Prove to them that you are aggressive.

FSBO Lead Templates

Although the leads that you'll receive from a good FSBO lead provider will be organized in some fashion, they are not set up for you to make calls most effectively. Usually they will be sent in a format containing the basic information that you'll need when calling. I would advise you to input all of the FSBO information from a lead provider into your FSBO Journal template. This guides your FSBO conversation and helps you with the essential questions and rankings for following up with your FSBOs.

CHAPTER 6

FSBO Sales Techniques

Don't be afraid to give your best to what seemingly are small jobs. Every time you conquer one it makes you that much stronger. If you do the little jobs well, the big ones will tend to take care of themselves.

—DALE CARNEGIE

FSBO Fact

Real estate professionals are experts in attracting qualified buyers. A broker or sales associate also can show a home more objectively than can a seller who may be emotionally attached to the home, and who might become unnerved by prospective buyers' critical comments. The real estate pro also checks the financial capability and bona fides of buyers before allowing them onto a seller's property.

SOURCE: National Association of Realtors®, *Profile of Home Buyers & Sellers,* 2005.

The best way to contact as many FSBOs as possible is by calling them one–by–one. You'll need to build rapport with the seller through conversation. You will also need to know when the opportunity is right to move in for the close. This is not a matter of timing but a matter of judgment. And lastly, you'll need to be able to sell your service to them better than your competition can. This requires you to know your service, believe in your service, and offer honest service.

Chapters 6 and 7 are the two most important chapters in this book. The majority of your time should be concentrated on calling FSBOs for appointments. In Chapter 6, we're going to go over the following elements:

- Preparing for the phone call
- Using questions to control the conversation
- Closing techniques
- Making the calls
- Three calls to the listing
- What to do after the call

Preparing for the Phone Call

The telephone can be very intimidating, but you have to get over this road block if you want to make money selling FSBOs. Before you make your first phone call you must be ready for every obstacle that a FSBO may throw at you. Not only that, but when you're first starting out it's hard to remember everything that you and your office offer when a FSBO demands an instant response from you.

Use the Power List

Here is what you need to do. Make a concise summary of everything your company and yourself offer. I call this your *Power List*. Include important characteristics that you posses that distinguishes you from the competition. Organize them in bullet points and have the list in sight for a quick-glance reference guide at times when you may need it fast. That way, when someone asks you a question such as, "Can you tell me about yourself and what you offer?" you can knock them dead with a steadfast response as if you've been doing this routine for years. Below are some ideas to get you thinking about your Power List.

Office Advantages

- Years your office has been in business
- Awards received by your office
- Number of agents in office
- Production record for your office
- Paper publications you advertise in
- Website advertisements
- Training your office provides for agents

Your Advantages

- Full-time agent
- Level of education (if pertinent)
- Aggressive sales approach
- Open house every Sunday
- Personal name rider on sign
- Competitive commission schedule

- Home warranty offer
- Direct mail advertisements blanketing the neighborhood
- Multiple pictures of home on the MLS
- FSBO specialist

I'm sure you can get the picture. The more you can list the better. The Power List is just for your own reference, but if you can recall all of your advantages from memory you'll really have an advantage. At a listing appointment you aren't allowed to bring your cheat sheet, so try to remember everything you offer.

Make Sure You Can Call

Before the call is made double-check on the MLS that the property is not already listed with another agent. Even though it may be a new ad, sometimes sellers list their home with the first agent who calls. This is why it is important to jump on new FSBO ads as soon as they are published.

If you *do* find that the property is already listed, scope out the agent that listed the home. This is your competition. You'll need to find out more about this agent. When you come in direct competition with this agent, be ready to show your prospect what you offer over that agent.

Check the Do Not Call Registry

Familiarize yourself with the Do Not Call Registry. Sure, many agents go around the Do Not Call List, but as an ethical agent you should follow the rules. Get a copy of the Do Not Call Registry from the Federal Trade Commission's website, www.donotcall.gov. You can receive names in up to five area codes free of charge; any additional area code will cost $25 per year. You can also take advantage of FSBO lead provider services, which offer leads that have been checked against doubles as well as against the Do Not Call List.

You can get around most of the Do Not Call rules if you're calling to say you have a buyer for the FSBOs property. FSBOs advertise their phone number to *buyers*, not agents. And technically, when FSBOs advertise their number to the public, they are inviting phone calls. If you have a buyer who fits some of the FSBOs selling criteria, you can call the FSBO and ask further questions to see if the home is a match for your client. If it's not a match, then ask if you can mail them your information or call back again at a later time. If they give you their approval, you can continue calling them.

Although it's not very common, the last thing you want to do is ruin your career by getting slapped with a $10,000 fine. So after you check the MLS and the Do Not Call Registry, you'll have all of the information from the ad in front of you to ask specific questions about the FSBO's property. Have your pen and FSBO Journal ready before you get started with the phone calls.

Start Your Calls Early

Start calling FSBOs in the morning until you run out of numbers to call. Some studies show that the best time to call homeowners is between 10 and 11 A.M. Yet some suggest the best time is between 6 and 8 P.M., simply because most people are home from work by that time. I say, they're both right. Regardless of studies, call FSBOs as soon, and as often, as possible. I would suggest starting no earlier than 10 A.M. and calling no later than 8 P.M. That leaves ten hours open every day for you to prospect.

Call from Home

Believe it or not, it's often better if you can prospect from home as opposed to calling from your office. This may go against what your broker tells you, but the reason your broker may want you to call from the office is to be sure you're not slacking off. If you are a slacker, then call from your office. At least you'll be under pressure from your broker to work.

The reason why it's better to prospect from home is because you need complete and total focus during such intimate calling sessions. It's also best to avoid distractions from other agents and office commotion when on the phone. Another reason why it's good to call from home is to have your name on the seller's caller ID (we get into this next).

If you can't get total focus from your home, you can go someplace where you'll have complete uninterrupted focus. Some offices have isolated rooms that you may be able to use. The objective here is to focus on your work without distractions.

Use Your Name for Caller ID

A very important reason not to call from the office is because your office name will show on the seller's caller ID. Thus, when you call FSBOs from your office, you're giving away that you're an agent *before* they even pick up the phone. You can try blocking the caller ID, but I'm sure FSBOs are used to getting calls from agents with blocked numbers, and many will not answer such calls.

Calling from your home number, especially when the phone is registered under your name, adds a personal touch to the call. When they see your name come up on the caller ID they won't know what to think. They'll know it's not a telemarketer, and they'll presume it's not a real estate office, so they're going to answer. When they pick up the phone and you identify yourself, the sellers will feel like you're an approachable person and will usually feel more comfortable with you. Not only that, but when you call with your name on the caller ID you are in essence advertising yourself on their phone. This is a great way to get your name stuck in their minds for later, when they make the decision to list. And by the way, if you don't have your phone registered in your name, look into doing this. These little things add up when you put them all together.

Using Questions to Control the Conversation

In order to get your prospect from point A to closing, you'll need to know how to guide them there.

Answer Questions with Questions

One of the best sales techniques used to control conversations is to answer a question with a question. This method is very useful because, first, from their point of view it doesn't look like you're trying to control the conversation. Second, it's easy to use.

It's simple . . . just answer a question with a question. Here's an example:

> **Seller:** "How much is your commission?"
> **Agent:** "Well, that depends. How much are you looking to invest in a professional?"

Here's another example of this technique:

> **Seller:** "Do you hold open houses?"
> **Agent:** "Would you like me to hold open houses for you?"

The concept of this technique is to keep you in the driver's seat and, at the same time it sets them up for minor closes. Once they answer your question, if they don't ask you a follow-up question, continue the questioning. Don't play Twenty Questions with them—that defeats the purpose. But you should ask them questions that guide. Here's another example so you can see how this technique can guide them to the close.

> **Seller:** "What's the length of your listing agreement?"
> **Agent:** "Well, that all depends on your motivation. How soon do you folks need to move?"

S: "We close on our new home in nine months."

A: "I shouldn't have a problem getting your home sold within nine months. Would you like me to put an expiration of nine months on the paperwork?"

S: "Well, I guess if you think you can sell it in that time . . . "

Did you catch what just happened? The conversation led from a simple average listing question to closing on the listing. This is a very simplified example, but I'm just trying to help you get to the core of why and how to use this.

Open-Ended Questions

As you have just seen, the person who asks the questions is the person in control of the conversation. To better show you how to stay in control, I am going to dissect the two types of questions you can ask while talking to a prospect. These are open-ended questions and closed-ended questions.

An *open-ended question* is what I call a "feeler question." It commands the prospect to give an answer that is typically lengthy and informative. The reason I call this a "feeler question" is because you use these types of questions to feel out the motives of the prospect when they answer.

To ask an open-ended question, you simply ask the question in a manner that requires a thoughtful answer, such as "Why are you moving?"

Here are the words to use when asking open-ended questions:

- Who?
- What?
- When?
- Where?
- Why?
- How?

Here are some examples of open-ended questions:

- "*What* locations are you thinking about moving to?"
- "*When* do you need to sell?"
- "*How* did you come up with the asking price for your home?"
- "*Why* are you folks selling?"

Closed-Ended Questions

Closed-ended questions, on the other hand, demand a "yes," no," or "maybe" response. The question is usually asked with a very specific objective in mind. For example:

Agent: "Do want to think it over?"
Seller: "No."

This type of question will give you a very specific response. But in order for you to get a "yes" instead of a "no," you'll need to include a tie-down, as we'll discuss in the next section.

Closing Techniques

In this game of selling, the main objective of your job is to close. You want to use tie-downs and minor closes with the seller in over-the-phone conversations, which lead up to the close for the appointment that can finally lead to a close for the listing. From there you hope to find a buyer and close on the sale. It's all about closing. For this section we are concentrating on closing for the appointment over the phone, which is the most important close that can take place while on the phone. This technique requires many minor closes that bring us to the major close. I will demonstrate all of the techniques required to achieve this aim.

Use Tie-Downs for the Minor Close

Here's how a tie-down works. Your objective is to close as early and as often as possible. Use tie-downs to close as many times as you may need to in order to commit to the final close, the close for the appointment.

A *tie-down* is a way of wording a question so that the prospect says "yes." Use a closed-ended question and, at the end of a sentence, place a tie-down to get a "yes" response. The objective here is to get your prospect to say "yes" as often as possible. Each "yes" you receive from the seller is a minor close. For example:

Agent: "Down the line if your home doesn't sell you will consider listing with an agent, *won't you?*"
Seller: "Yes."

The "won't you" was the tie-down at the end of the sentence, and the "yes" was a minor close. Here are some of the terms used for tie-downs:

Aren't they?	Don't we?	Won't you?
Aren't you?	Shouldn't we?	Isn't it?
Can't you?	Wouldn't it?	Isn't that right?
Doesn't it?	Don't you agree?	Didn't it?
Couldn't it?	Hasn't he?	Haven't they?
Wasn't it?	Hasn't she?	Won't they?

Using the same terms, tie-downs can also be in the beginning of sentences. For example:

Agent: *"Won't it* look nice once you have all of your furniture in place?"
Seller: *"Yes."*

Another way to use tie-downs is to place them in the middle of the sentence. Here's an example:

Agent: *"With all of the marketing we do for you, won't you agree* that you'll increase your odds of selling?"
Seller: *"Yes."*

There are many ways to phrase tie-downs. The bottom line is that they must be questions for which the only answer can be a "yes" or one of its many derivatives. Depending on the conversation, pick which type of tie-down and what placement will work best. Practice using tie-downs so they become second nature to you. This is a strong sales technique that is especially important when calling FSBOs.

Here is a sample dialogue to illustrate using tie-downs in a phone conversation to get the prospect into the habit of saying "yes." I'm going to shorten the conversation to give you the important parts of this lesson.

> **Agent:** "Hi, this is [Your Name] with [Your Company] Realty, how are you?"
>
> **Seller:** "Good, how can I help you?"
>
> **A:** "I notice you're selling a two-bedroom, two-bath loft on Division Street. How many square feet is this property?"
>
> **S:** "It's 1,200 square feet, why do you want to know?"
>
> **A:** "We'll, I'm just updating my records of unlisted homes in your area. Your property is for sale by owner, *isn't it?*"
>
> **S:** "*Yes*, for now."
>
> **A:** "For now? So you're going to list at some point, *aren't you?*"
>
> **S:** "*Yes*, at some point, if we can't sell on our own, we will list with an agent."
>
> **A:** "I see . . . If I told you that you could be costing yourself thousands of dollars, *would you* consider listing your home sooner?"
>
> **S:** "If that's true, then, *yes*."
>
> **A:** "A 2006 national study shows that the average for sale by owner home sold for $59,800 less than with agent-assisted homes. *Won't you agree* that this is a lot of money?"
>
> **S:** "*Yes.*"

Each "yes" you receive from the prospect is a minor close. The more "yeses" you get brings you closer to the final close: the listing appointment, and ultimately the listing. You'll slowly but surely refine this technique until it becomes part of your language.

The Alternative-Choice Close

An alternative-choice close is a technique that asks for the close by giving alternative options from which the prospects can choose. Thereby, when prospects pick one of the alternatives they essentially agree with the close.

Here's a basic example of an alternative-choice close out of context: "Which one is your favorite color, red or blue?" The person asked this question may have black as their favorite color, but when asked to pick one from the two choices they will state that their favorite color is either red or blue. Here is another example, but this time it's put into context of the real estate business:

> **Agent:** "I would like to show you what I have to offer. We could meet tomorrow at 3 P.M., or would 5 P.M. work better for you?"

The sellers don't at first have to agree with meeting tomorrow, but when asked to pick from two alternative choices, they feel the need to pick one, and in essence agree to close for the appointment.

This is an example of how to use your tie-downs and alternative-choice closes in the context you'll encounter and then how to step in for the final close. The final close is not about timing. It is about your judgment of when the seller is most willing to consider your close. You have to be able to feel out the seller. That comes with getting to know them just based on an over-the-phone conversation. Once you get to know them and their motivations, you'll be able to determine what time is right to close.

Common Closing Mistakes

Closing requires many delicate procedures. You have learned the basic closing techniques. Now, to better prepare you to close your prospect, here is a list of what you should avoid:

- Talking too much
- Not asking questions
- Avoiding the problem
- Not listening to your seller
- Being unprepared
- Not asking for the close!

Making the Calls

Now, with all of the tools you have so far, you're ready to start calling FSBOs effectively. Remember, keep your FSBO Journal out with a pen, your Power List, and some FSBO mailing packages ready to be addressed, stamped, and handed to your mailperson for a speedy delivery. You must try to be the best and the most aggressive agent in the area. That's why a speedy mail delivery is important.

Typical Calls

Now I'm going to give you some examples of different dialogues you may encounter when calling FSBOs. These are shortened to spare you the needless details. Here are a few scenarios that you may experience. You should familiarize yourself with these as much as you can. You'll have conversations that are good, bad, and everything in between, so keep in mind that these dialogue examples are not the only scenarios you'll face when calling FSBOs. Pay attention to the next dialogue set examining a typical conversation with a FSBO.

The typical phone call to a FSBO goes something like this:

Agent: "Hi, this is [Your Name] with [Your Company] Realty. I'm calling about the home for sale on Brown Street . . . is it still available?

Seller: "Yes."

A: "How many bedrooms and bathrooms does it have?"

S: "Three bedrooms and two bathrooms."

A: "Does it have a garage?"

S: "Yes, a two-car garage."

A: "Wonderful, and how much are you asking?"

S: "$349,900."

A: "That sounds fair, let me ask you something. If I had a buyer, would you work with me as a buyer's agent?"

S: "What does that mean?"

A: "Well, typically, if I find a home for my buyer through the Multiple Listing Service I would expect a co-op brokerage fee of 2.5 percent . . . is that something you would consider if I found a buyer for your home?"

S: "Well sure, if that's all."

A: "OK, great! Let me ask you this. Have you ever considered professionally marketing your home?"

S: "You mean with an agent?"

A: "Yes."

S: "Yeah, we thought about it but we're not ready yet."

A: "Well, is it okay if I mail you my business card? That way you can keep it on file for when you decide to go that route. [Remember to mail the FSBO Package, not just your business card.]

S: "Sure."

A: "Before I go, I just want to ask you one more question. Are you aware that 87 percent of transactions involve a Realtor?"

S: "No."

A: "That means that you're only exposing your home to 13 percent of the buyers on the market. That's not very much exposure, *is it*?"

S: "I guess not, but we're not looking to pay a 5 percent commission."

A: "Mr. Seller, let me bring up one more point if I may. According to the 2006 study from the National Association of Realtors, nationwide, you receive an average of 32 percent more at closing when you sell your home with an agent versus by owner. That significantly outweighs the brokerage fee, *doesn't it*?"

S: "Well, send me your information and I'll talk it over with my wife."

A: "Sure thing, and is it okay if I follow up in a few days to make sure you received my mailing?"

S: "Yeah, that's okay."

[Now place a call-back date in your FSBO Journal.]

A: "Perfect, Mr. Seller. Just in case you decide to get started in the meantime, I'll give you my contact information so you have it available. *Do you have a pen ready?*"

S: "Yes."

Keep in mind you do not want to come off as a "pushy salesperson." After the conversation, mark on your FSBO Journal when you feel is the best time to follow up. Typically with a seller like this, I would follow up in three to four days. Try to time your follow-up call with the mail delivery of your FSBO Package. Record your conversation details, and mark this particular seller as "warm" because he has good potential. This would be a Class A FSBO—those who think they can save money by selling themselves because they evidently don't know that's not true.

Send the seller your resume, the FSBO statistics that you mentioned in the conversation, your business card, and a refrigerator magnet (if you have them). Then plan to follow up in three to four business days. Also include a note in the envelope with a personal statement in your handwriting. You can write something along these lines:

Mr. Seller,

It was a pleasure speaking with you on Tuesday.

If you need someone aggressive to guide your transaction, give me a call.

Best of luck,
[Your Name]

When you call them back, introduce yourself again because FSBOs get a lot of phone calls from agents. Ask them if they received your information that you mailed them. Here is some sample dialogue for a follow-up call:

Agent: "Hi, this is [Your Name] with [Your Company] Realty. We spoke last Tuesday about your home for sale."
Seller: "Yes, hi."
A: "I mailed you some information about me and what I offer, did you receive it?"
S: "Yes, we received it."
A: "Well, have you given any thought to having a professional market your home?"
S: "Yes, we have."
[Then they usually have various questions to ask you about what you offer.]

Here is your window of opportunity. You should go over, concisely, everything you offer. Remember to look at your Power List, and include any guarantees you may be able to make. Guarantees really hit hard, it's a sure thing for them. Use your tie-downs and then close for the appointment.

Ask them if you can meet with them in person to preview their home. If you close for the listing appointment, get prepared to answer any and all questions at the seller's home. We'll get into the listing appointment in Chapter 8.

The Easy Seller

Every once in a while you do get an easy seller, as shown by the following dialogue:

Agent: "Hi, this is [Your Name] with [Your Company] Realty. I'm calling about the home for sale on Brown Street . . . is it still available?"

Seller: "Yes, it is, how can I help you?"

A: "How many bedrooms and bathrooms does this home have?"

S: "We have three bedrooms and two baths."

A: "Does it have a garage?"

S: "Yes, a new two-car garage with an automatic door."

A: "Wonderful, and how much are you asking?"

S: "We're *asking* $349,900, but it's negotiable."

A: "You mean, you aren't firm on your price?"

S: "Right, we need to sell this house ASAP."

A: "Ok. Let me ask you something. If you need to sell ASAP, why are you selling by owner?"

S: "Because we wanted to try it out and see what happens."

A: "I see. Well, if I can prove to you that selling by owner will leave you with 32 percent less in your pocket at closing, *would you consider a new approach?*"

S: "Absolutely, we are open to options."

A: "If you don't mind, I would like to see your home and tell you exactly what we can offer that can sell your home ASAP and get you top dollar...*would that be ok?*"

S: "Yeah, I need to sell, so let's see what we can do."

A: "I can make it there by 3 P.M., or would 6 P.M. be better for you?"

At this point you're closing for the appointment. Fill out most of the listing agreement and disclosures before you get to the appointment. That way, there's no awkward silence while you're filling out the paperwork.

Calling a FSBO rarely goes as smoothly as in this example, but it does happen. You just have to pick up the phone, make the calls, and you *will* see results.

Leave a Message

If you're wondering what to do when you get a seller's voicemail, you're not alone. The answer is, *leave a message!* You shouldn't leave the same seller a message every single time you call, but maybe once or twice. You *will* get calls back. And when they *do* call you back, ANSWER YOUR PHONE! So many agents will call and leave messages for sellers, but when it comes time to step up to the plate when they call back, they back down. Just to help you out with some dialogue, here is an example of a message you can leave the FSBO on their answering machine:

> **Agent:** "Hi, this is [Your Name] with [Your Company] Realty. I'm calling about the property for sale on Belmont. I would like some information about the property to give to my buyers. You can reach me at 555-5555, again that's 555-5555. I look forward to hearing from you. Have a great day."

Notice that I said the phone number twice. You should always do this if you are leaving your number on an answering machine. Either your phone or their phone might start to get static and distort one or two of your numbers, then you'll definitely never hear back from them. Here's how the dialogue may go when a FSBO returns your call later that evening:

> **Seller:** "Hi, you left me a message on my phone requesting information about my home for sale."
>
> **Agent:** "Yes, thank you for returning my call. I called a *few* properties for sale. Can you tell me the address of the home you're selling?"
>
> **S:** "123 Belmont."
>
> **A:** "Right, well, I have a few questions about your property."
>
> [Then you can go into the routine that we just discussed that involves questioning the seller to feel out their character and motivations.]

Three Calls to the Listing

On average, you'll find that it will take about three phone calls, if done properly, to get the seller to give you a listing appointment. The steps should follow an order as shown in the chart below. The following section outlines what each step entails.

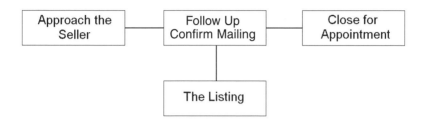

Figure 6-1. Three calls to the listing.

Call 1. Approach the Seller

The first phone call that actually connects you to the seller is going to be the toughest one to close. At first, you will be just another agent who is trying to get the seller's listing. This is the most important phone call because it sets the stage for what is to come in future phone calls with this seller.

Here is an outline of how the first phone call to the seller should proceed:

1. State your name and introduce yourself.
2. Start by asking some "feeler questions" about the home.
3. Get their mailing address and mention that you

will be sending them your information (the FSBO Package).

4. State your name again when ending the phone call.

Call 2. Follow Up

The second phone call is typically a follow-up call. This will take place about three to four days after the first phone call, depending on the mail delivery speed in your area. It's best to try and call sellers right when they get the FSBO Package, so that you're fresh in their mind. Confirm that they received your mailing and work from there.

This is how the second call may go:

1. State your name and introduce yourself.
2. Mention that you spoke with them a few days ago.
3. Confirm that they received the information that you mailed them.
4. Ask them what they thought about the information.
5. Using minor closes, try to lead the conversation to the close for the appointment.
6. Let them know when you'll call back to follow up.
7. State your name again as you end the phone call.

Each phone call will go in its own direction. If you feel that you can close for the listing appointment on the second or even first phone call, by all means do it. Use your closing techniques to gain control of the conversation, which will leave the seller thinking about what you've just discussed. The next time you call, the seller should be ready for the listing appointment.

Call 3. Close for the Appointment

This may very well be your last phone call before the listing appointment. If that's the case, here is what to do in this phone conversation:

1. State your name and introduce yourself.
2. Recap on what you spoke about in the last phone conversation.
3. Use minor closes to lead back to the listing appointment.
4. Close for the listing appointment using an alternative-choice close.
5. Thank them for giving you this opportunity.
6. Confirm the appointment time again.

Now that you've closed for the listing appointment, you'll need to get ready for the listing presentation. Refer to Chapter 8 for how best to prepare for the listing presentation.

What to Do After the Call

Follow Up with a Mailing

Have copies of your resume, business cards, and envelopes ready to be addressed and mailed to FSBOs right after you finished talking with them. The best thing you can do is mail these out that same day if possible. What I advise you to do is ask your mail delivery person if they will pick up your outgoing mail for you. If so, you can just stuff and address your mail and put it in your own mailbox to be delivered as soon as possible. There's nothing better than fast service to a FSBO. It helps when you call them back a few days later and ask, "Did you receive my mail?" and they say, "Yes, we did." Then you've got a foot in the door because now they remember you, and they know you mean business.

Follow Up with Pending FSBOs

If you called a FSBO who says that they just accepted an offer, keep following up with them. Studies show that on average 10 percent of home sales get canceled for one reason or another. That means that these are still good prospects to follow up with.

Don't follow up as often as you would with your usual prospects but enough to keep yourself in the picture should their pending sale start to fall through. Ask the seller when the sale is expected to close and call back two weeks before the closing; then call again one week before closing, until they close. If that 10 percent rate holds true, then your odds of listing the property, should they choose an agent, would be close to 100 percent. Chances are, when the transaction goes south, you'll be the only agent who actually followed up.

Visit FSBO Open Houses

While you call FSBOs during the week, ask them whether they're holding an open house on Sunday. Then, on Sunday, have your FSBO Packages ready and hit as many as you can. Remember, it's a numbers game, the more you hit the better your odds are. After each visit to an open house, mail a Thank You card to that seller thanking them for allowing you to view their home. Keep pre-stamped cards in your car so you can mail them after each open house you visit. That way, they'll get the cards lightning fast, which will make a good impression.

Here is a sample Thank You card to use for your FSBO open house follow-up mailing:

Dear Seller,

It was a pleasure meeting you. I want to thank you for taking the time to show me your wonderful home. You know, hiring an agent can earn you 32 percent more for your property. Keep me in mind if you would like to maximize your net proceeds at closing.

Here are some homes we recently sold in your neighborhood:

- 523 Main Street
- 555 Washington Avenue
- 1100 Chestnut Drive
- 576 Adams Street
- 1200 Peachtree Lane

Respectfully,
[Your Name]
[Your Company]

If you already have listings that have scheduled open houses, you can ask another agent from your office to sit the open house while you're out visiting FSBO open houses. Depending on the market, you may be able to procure more leads on a FSBO open house hunt than sitting your own open house. Any agent who doesn't have an open house to sit should be up for the job. If not, try offering to do all of the leg work for the agent, such as installing the signs and printing brochures.

In this chapter, we've discussed many sales approaches that you'll need to refine through practice. In the next chapter we will cover additional phone techniques and delve into objection handling.

CHAPTER 7

Special Telephone Techniques

Failure is the only opportunity to begin again, only this time more wisely.

—Unknown Author

FSBO Fact

In 2006, just 12 percent of sellers chose the FSBO route, down from 13 percent the previous year, according to NAR's 2006 statistics. This number is down from about 20 percent in 1987.

Source: National Association of Realtors®,
Profile of Home Buyers & Sellers, 2006.

In this chapter we will cover some useful tips and many special techniques you can employ when dealing with FSBOs by phone, including:

- Communicating effectively
- Handling objections

- Dealing with tough sellers
- Discussing fees, discounts, and incentives

Communicating Effectively

Learning to communicate professionally and effectively over the phone is well within your reach. When talking on the phone you have to remember that the seller can't see you. Give them as much of a professional and experienced image as you can through just your voice and tone.

The tone of your voice indicates to the seller your mood and motivations. If they perceive you as a pushy salesperson by the sound of your voice, they won't give you the time of day to go further with a conversation. Try to vary the tone of your voice while speaking. Practice your speech by recording yourself speaking in different situations and playing it back to find what you can improve on. You can also practice using your vocal cords so that they are in tune when you use them. Start by humming the lowest note you can for three seconds and gradually increase the tone higher and higher every three seconds. This will help you move the tone of your voice up and down smoothly without creating awkward sounds in between.

Common Communication Mistakes

1. *Ego arguments.* Many of us have, at times, regretted something we've said in the past. It may have been out of bad temper or to prove a point.

Nonetheless, getting into a verbal argument with a prospect will only feed the real estate agent stereotype in their mind. The last thing you want to do is create an awkward or hostile situation with a seller just because you want to satisfy your own self-desire to prove a point. Whether it be politics, religion (which you should never discuss with clients), or if you just can't get a seller to grasp the concept that you are trying to relay, DO NOT let your ego get in the way. You will only lose prospects and end up weaker than your competition. Remember the old saying, "Don't win the battle and lose the war." So leave your ego at the door when calling FSBOs.

2. *Ask for the appointment.* So you specified to the FSBO what you and your office has to offer, and you gave your verbal presentation . . . now what? Ask for the appointment!! Many agents will wait for the seller to ask for the appointment, but the seller never will. If you feel that they are on the same page as you, and have a good feeling about closing for the appointment, then do it. Asking for the close is very important because if you don't ask, you won't close, bottom line. Don't be shy. Ask for what you want in life. You'll be surprised at what you receive.

3. *Don't talk too much.* For those of you who love to talk, keep it within reason. Many of us get excited when we find that the seller is interested in

what we have to say. Don't let that excitement come out in the form of overly exuberant talking. If you have a good thing going, don't milk it. You'll only lose the seller's interest and ultimately lose the listing.

Effective Communication Techniques

1. *Smile.* Smiling displays your enthusiasm. While talking on the phone, people on the other end often can hear the tone of your voice change when you smile. This gives them the mental image that you are, in fact, smiling. Smiling shows that you are sincere and confident in yourself. And if you're confident in yourself, sellers will develop confidence in you. So, smile often.

2. *Speak clearly.* In order for you to prevent the seller from awkwardly asking "What did you say?" you must be able to speak clearly and pronounce all of your syllables effectively. You can practice by reading a book out loud and exercising your mouth, tongue, and lips, to say words precisely how they should be pronounced. Also, try tongue twisters, which will help you speak using all syllables. People cannot read your lips over the phone so you need to be able to communicate clearly.

3. *Don't use laymen's words.* To sound professional, avoid words like "uh," "umm," "like," and

"yeah." Replace them with words like "well" and "yes." Don't use the word "like" in this way: "I'm like the best agent in town." That is a poor use of the word and makes you sound inexperienced and uneducated. Also, avoid words that spark negative feelings. Negative words trigger bad thoughts. For example, instead of using the word "cost," say "investment." Here is a list of negative words and some suggestions on how to replace them:

Negative Word	*Replacement*
Cost or Price	Investment
Deal or Sold	Transaction
Commission	Brokerage Fee
Signature or Sign	Approve or Approval
Contract or Listing Agreement	Paperwork

Don't these replacement words sound less negative? Rehearse these words so they become part of your vocabulary when it comes time to use them.

4. *Identify yourself.* You're a real estate agent, not an actor. Some agents act like they are buyers when they call FSBOs and then at the last moment inform the seller that they are an agent. Not only is this bad business ethics, but you come off as sneaky and completely untrustworthy. If you identify yourself as an agent right away, they'll

know that you're honest and at least not trying to act like you're a buyer. When calling FSBOs the last thing you want to do is be sneaky. Remember this: FSBOs get more calls from agents than buyers. Therefore, they can tell a buyer from an agent. Don't play dumb because they'll call you out and make you wish you had never called.

Listening

One quality you'll soon discover in people is that they like to talk about themselves and what they have achieved. In order for you to be able to feel out the personality and motivations of your prospect, you'll have to be a good listener. Think about it, what do most people enjoy talking about the most? The answer is, themselves. This remains true for many social conversations, whether it be dating, storytelling, or proving a point. For FSBOs, the conversation may be about themselves and also about what they have done with their home in terms of improvements and customizations. So, when they go off on a tangent on how they remodeled the bathrooms and the kitchen . . . *LISTEN!*

This is also a relationship tool. You have to listen to people if you want to be listened to. If you can't listen to the seller, they are going to get agitated. And nothing is worse than a salesperson who talks over a prospect because they want to take their turn in boasting about themselves. That will shoot needles into your seller's nerves. Do not talk over people. The best thing to do is, listen for a break and then step into the conversation and do your part.

Listening is the best way to get to know a seller. Many times, if you listen long enough, a seller will spill their guts and reveal their deepest motivations. Write down as much of the important information as you can. The more you listen, the closer you get with that seller and the closer they'll feel toward you. You'll be able to better judge when to move in for the close when you listen to a seller long enough to understand them.

What happens when you get a seller who doesn't stop talking? Honestly, if you have the time, let them talk to you until they are blue in the face. Chances are, you'll make a new friend, and they'll be open to your attempt to close for the appointment. But if you really need to get on to that next call, then wait for a break in the conversation and just say, "Great, well, I'm going to mail you my info, and why don't I follow up with you in a few days and see how things are going?" Be courteous and creative but don't be rude.

Handling Objections

If you are not familiar with objection handling techniques, then this is important information for your success in this career. For those of you who understand objection handling, you'll learn some new tips in this section.

The techniques used in this section of the chapter should help you handle objections effectively and convert objections into minor closes, which will pave the way to the final close. It is important that you stay in control of the conversation and follow up, follow up, follow up!

You will have to face objections in two circumstances, before they occur and as they occur. If you're facing objections before they occur, that means that you are having problems with intimidation or the fear of rejection. The best remedy for this is to learn by trial and error. Start to get an idea of what objections are out there for you to climb over and then create a plan to counter them.

Objection Action Plan

There are only so many objections that a FSBO can throw at you. Think of all of the possible objections that you can, and write them down on a piece of paper. Then think of all of the possible counters to those objections you can and write them down next to the objections. Now you can use these to practice your minor closes and tie-downs when faced with these objections.

Convert Objections

Use minor closes when countering objections. These are ways in which you can turn a prospect's uncertainty into an agreement. Simply by countering your prospect's objection with an answer then a question, you can get them moving in the right direction, to the final close.

Here are some examples of converting objections into minor closes:

> **Seller:** "We think that a 5 percent commission is too much."
>
> **Agent:** "Sometimes investing in a professional does seem intimidating. But, if I showed you how that 5 percent

investment gives you a 640 percent return on your money, *then would you be interested?"*

S: "I'd be interested, but I want to know how that is possible."

[You then refer to your FSBO Statistics sheet for the details on the current return on your investment for your market.]

Did you see how that worked? Let's try another example:

Seller: "We're not interested in using a real estate agent right now."

Agent: "Many of us *do* take pride and personal satisfaction by accomplishing things ourselves. If I could prove to you, without a shadow of a doubt, that you're costing yourself more money selling your home by owner than using an agent, *would you consider hiring a professional?"*

And another example:

Seller: "Bring me a buyer and I'll pay you a commission."

Agent: "You'll be first on my mind when I find a buyer that fits your home. But, Mr. Seller, I specialize in marketing and selling real estate. If I had a buyer for every house on the market I'd be a billionaire. What I *can* do is bring more buyers through your door, which will increase your odds of selling and maximize your sales price. *Wouldn't that interest you?"*

And here is one last example:

Seller: "We want to wait until spring to list our home with an agent."

Agent: "Spring *is* a great time for selling a home. If I showed you how you can sell your property faster *now* than in the spring, *would you consider listing today?*"

S: "I don't think that's possible, but if you can do that I'll consider it."

Then you can go into an answer of your choice (for some good ideas to counter with, refer to the section below). You can tell them that having a sign up in front of their home is essentially adding market time onto their property and that listing today will stop their home from becoming stale. Be as creative and influential as possible. Write down the responses to as many objections you can think of and practice using them in real conversation scenarios. That way you'll build your reflex to answering these like a pro.

Common Objections and Counters

If you are like most agents, objection handling is probably one of your biggest weaknesses. Here are some common objections you'll face and some ideas for countering the objections:

Objection: "We don't want to list in winter."
Counters:

- "In the winter weather people still shop for homes and those that are looking are more serious."

- "Many jobs get relocated in winter. These workers need a place to live."
- "Fewer homes are listed in winter so there is less competition against your home."
- "Holiday decorations can give your house a comfortable down-home feel. This will create an experience that buyers will look forward to recreating."
- "You will be ahead of the influx of spring listings by selling your home now."

Objection: "I have someone in the family who is an agent."

Counters:

- "You know, sometimes hiring a friend or relative will put you at risk of damaging your relationship should things go sour with the transaction."
- "You may be overlooking important characteristics in this agent that you would otherwise not have if you hired someone you didn't already know."
- "It's hard to fire a friend or relative when things go bad."

Objection: "I already have a buyer for my home."

Counters:

- "If you already have one buyer while advertising your home by owner, imagine how many buyers you would have if you had your home listed through a professional with ten times more market exposure."
- "Chances are, if you already have a buyer for your home, you are selling it under value."

- "Even though you may have a buyer, you should have a professional qualify the buyer, negotiate the highest price on your behalf, and handle all of the paperwork that is involved."

Objection: "We found an agent that will list our home for less commission."
Counters:
- "Many agents that give discounts are really taking the discount out on the buyer agents, which reduces your activity."
- "If you're getting a discount, you're probably not getting the marketing that you deserve and that we provide."
- "Someone who discounts themselves will not have as much incentive to work as hard as me."
- "Remember that old saying; you get what you pay for."

Turn Objections into Benefits

One way of turning the tables on an objection is to convert it into a benefit. By converting the objection into a benefit, you convert the negative feelings associated with it into positive ones, as shown in the following example:

Seller: "We think the commission is too high."
Agent: "That is exactly why you should consider me as your agent."
S: "Please explain."

A: "Well, if you needed brain surgery, you wouldn't go to the cheapest surgeon, would you?"

S: "No."

A: "Well, with your largest investment being your home, you should treat it in the same fashion, wouldn't you agree?"

S: "Yes."

A: "Then investing in a professional to market your home makes sense, *doesn't it?*"

S: "Yes."

Now the seller associates this brokerage fee with doing what is right for the home. You have turned an objection into a benefit for the seller. This can easily be done as long as you are well prepared for the objections that you may face. Get to know objections and the different approaches to use in order to convert them into benefits. Practice the counters until you can convert every objection into a benefit.

Objection handling requires practice to master. In your spare time, rehearse your techniques to better your skills. The best teacher in life is experience, so if you really want to increase your ability to handle objections, get on the phone and start learning.

Dealing with Tough Sellers

With some sellers, you may find it difficult to strike up a good relationship. You will get the occasional FSBO who is rough around the edges, does not show any personality, and is cold when dealing with agents. When you encounter such sellers, just play along. The one thing that you never want to do is create tension by pushing your objectives on them. Even if you don't agree with something they say, many times you just have to bite your tongue and resist putting in your two cents on the subject. In order to win over a seller like this, it will take a bit more patience and perseverance than usual. You have to prove to them that you won't give up on them (like most agents probably have done already), even though their attitude may be hard to deal with. There will be good occasions for you to slip in your tie-downs and get some minor closes.

Be Patient and Follow Up

Even if the phone conversation goes bad, set a time in your FSBO Journal to call them back and *stick to it*. With tough sellers, the follow-up calls will be further apart at first, say five to eight days, which you then can narrow down to around three to five days apart as the sellers become more comfortable with you.

You'll see that many of these sellers will turn around. You may be shocked when you are able to list some tough FSBOs, on whom you were about to give up. Why is that? That's because you have virtually no competition. All of the other agents have moved on because they are intimidated by tough sellers. But when that seller realizes that they need an agent, who will come to mind? *You!*

Here is a sample dialogue from a tough seller:

Agent: "Hi, this is [Your Name] with [Your Company] Realty. I'm calling about the home for sale on Brown Street . . . is it still available?"

Seller: "Yeah, why? Do you have a buyer?"

A: "Well, I *am* working with several buyers in your area but I don't know enough about your home to tell if this is what my buyers are looking for. Can I ask you some questions about your home?"

S: "I don't want to work with a real estate agent."

A: "Ms. Seller, we do a lot of production in your area. The reason I'm calling is to take down information about your property as a home for sale by owner. That way, if I *can't* find my buyer a home on the MLS, I just may call you. *Does that sound fair?*"

S: "What do you want to know?"

A: "Well, how many bedrooms and bathrooms do you have?"

S: "Three bedrooms, two baths."

A: "Is this a brick or a frame home?"

S: "Brick."

A: "And what is the asking price?"

S: "$349,900."

A: "Sounds fair, can I ask you why you're selling by owner?"

S: "We're not paying an agent $17,000."

A: "I see . . . "

[At this point, I wouldn't start with the statistics. They can still be won over but it's not going to be on the first call. This type of seller has set up a large defense barrier between her and you as an agent. It's going to take patience and understanding to take down those barriers.]

A: "Well, Ms. Seller, I would like to mail you my business card just in case you need some advice or help down the road, *would that be okay?*"

S: "I guess."

A: "This is your mailing address, *isn't it?*"

When you follow up in a few days, they should be a bit more relaxed with you because they are familiar with you, but that's not always the case. It may take a few follow-up calls to completely break down the defense barriers for a tough seller, but once it's done, you can continue with the close for the appointment and get the listing.

Be Persistent

Even if the seller is rude, and I mean *RUDE,* do not give up on them. Selling a home is often very frustrating and overwhelming. If you show that you are persistent and understanding it will pay off in the long run when *they* give up.

Here's a story that I use as a great example on why you shouldn't give up on the tough ones. One of my tough FSBO sellers, whom we'll call Stacy for this story, had almost convinced me to give up on her. The first time I called her I said, "Hi, this is John Maloof . . . " but then, before I could finish, she butted in and said, "#@*! off!", excuse my language, and hung up on me. I asked myself, "Should I keep this FSBO in my Journal or just cross her off right now?" Well, with discipline, I kept her in the FSBO Journal and continued to follow up, follow up, and follow up. I received the same response from Stacy time after time. But one day, unexpectedly, she *called me!* She asked for an appointment to meet me and list her house.

What was the reason, you may ask? According to Stacy, I sounded nice over the phone and I wasn't pushy like the "other" agents. I will bet that all of the other agents gave up on her after the first phone call, just like I almost did. Needless to say, I got the listing and many more using the same discipline, which is *following up*. The moral of that story is, *DO NOT GIVE UP!*

Visit FSBOs Who Don't Answer

If you find yourself calling some FSBOs over three times without getting an answer, then visit them in person. Start by making a list of all the FSBOs that won't answer the phone or return messages. Prepare your FSBO packages beforehand and make your rounds. Some of these sellers may have already sold. But a number of them may just be too busy to handle the sale of their home. These are the ones that we're looking for.

The best part about this task is that you barely have any competition against you. The reason for this is that most agents will give up calling a FSBO if they don't get an answer on the first try. Not only that, but an even smaller number of agents, if any at all, will visit them in person, like you're doing.

When you visit the home of the FSBO, the dialogue may go something like this:

Agent: "Hi, I'm [your name] with [Your Company] Realty, I called you a couple of times for information about your home for sale. It's still available, *isn't it?*

Seller: "Yes, it's still for sale."

A: "Great. I stopped by to ask a couple of questions about the property, *would that be okay with you?*"

S: "Sure."

[Then ask some questions about the property that aren't mentioned in the advertisement.]

A: "I'm sure that you're a busy homeowner. Have you considered marketing your home with a professional?"

S: "We thought about it, but we don't know if we're ready yet."

A: "Well, I'm going to leave you with my information. That way you can think about your options and call me when you're ready to go that route, *does that sound all right with you?*"

S: "Yeah, I'll call you if I decide to list."

A: "Fantastic. I can stop by again to follow up with your progress or would you prefer me to call?"

S: "You can call me."

A: "Since it was difficult for me to reach you on the number advertised, can I have a direct number where you can be reached?"

Now you have your foot in the door with this seller, and you have a number for the seller that no other agent has. Call the seller back in two days and try to close for the listing appointment. Focus on the service aspect of listing with you. This type of seller will need someone to handle the listing because they are just too busy.

Discussing Fees, Discounts, and Incentives

Justify Your Brokerage Fee

According to NAR, 53 percent of sellers choose to sell "by owner" because they don't want to pay a brokerage fee. By and large, the brokerage fee is going to be the most common argument you'll face when calling FSBOs.

Seven Tips for Justifying Your Brokerage Fee

1. Selling FSBO versus selling through a real estate agent costs the seller on average 32 percent at closing. If you do the math, based on a 5 percent brokerage fee the seller receives over 640 percent return on their investment in an agent. This is the single best factor you can acknowledge.

2. Eighty-seven percent of homes sold are through the MLS. Without the MLS, FSBOs will experience significantly less market exposure.

3. Real estate agents have been through many transactions and have the know-how to deal with the paperwork and legal ramifications that come with selling a property, unlike sellers who may have experienced only a handful of transactions over their lifetime.

4. Without an experienced negotiator acting as the buffer between the seller and the buyer, the home may sell for less than its potential.

5. Real estate offices have the advertising tools to easily expose their property to buyers. This includes advertisement contracts with newspapers and Internet firms. Also, a brand-name real estate office handling the transaction provides reassurance that the transaction will go smoothly.

6. Selling a home by owner requires tremendous time and footwork, all of which an agent is willing to take on.

7. Without the MLS, sellers will not be able to create an accurate market analysis. This will lead to an overpriced or underpriced home. Either way, this is not good.

Offer Discounts and Incentives

Saving money is first and foremost on a FSBO's agenda. You can bet that you'll be faced with the obstacle of handling a discount request from your sellers. Follow your seven tips for justifying your brokerage fee. If the topic of a discount seems to creep back into the conversation, then here is some advice.

There are several ways to handle the discount problem. Your brokerage fee is negotiable. If you are open to the idea of discounting your fee, it's up to you how far you're willing to come down. However, whatever you ultimately agree upon with the seller, make sure it's in writing.

- *Dual Agency Discount.* Offer to list the property at full price but also tell them that if you sell the home yourself as a dual agent (when you are both the buyer and seller's agent) you will discount the brokerage fee for them. Dual agency is rare. This is usually the safest way to offer a discount.

- *Temporary Discount.* Give them a temporary discount. How this works is simple. For the first two weeks of your listing, tell your seller that if the property sells you'll discount the brokerage fee. After the two-week period expires, the full fee will go into effect.

  This is typically done when you or your office plan on spending a heavy amount of money on the marketing of your listing. After time, the marketing can add up and eat into the overall brokerage fee that you will be receiving. But if you sell the property in the first two weeks, you'll be saving on the marketing.

- *Incentives.* Throw in some incentives to make up for a discount in the brokerage fee. For example, you can offer to pay for a one-year home warranty and a virtual tour of the property. These still cost you, but it shouldn't be nearly as much as the discount the seller may have in mind.

- *Future Discount.* Tell the seller that if you get an offer that really stretches their bottom-line, you can negotiate a discount with the cooperating agent. Then when you receive an offer through another agent, you can negotiate with that agent to reduce their brokerage fee and help get the offer accepted. Once the agent is already in the door with his buyers, he can't walk away from your request. He'll have to consider it. If the cooperating agent decides not to negotiate the brokerage fee, then you can offer to split the discount with him. Most of the time, the seller won't even mention your future discount offer by the time an offer comes through.

- *Verbal Cancellation Listing.* Offering a verbal cancellation listing agreement can outweigh most discounts that you encounter. This type of listing agreement has no expiration date and can be canceled verbally by the seller at any time. The seller will almost always take you up on this offer because there are no strings attached and they are not "locked in" to a contract with you for a long period of time.

  The reason why this is to your advantage is because the seller rarely cancels the listing with you on their own. I've had sellers suggest a three-month listing and light up with excitement when I suggest a verbal cancellation listing. The listing would then go well beyond the initial three months that they suggested. Why is that, you say? When there is an expiration date, they don't have to fire anyone . . . you're fired automatically. The reason that the seller doesn't cancel with a verbal cancellation listing is because they feel uncomfortable firing you, or they may be satisfied with the job you are doing for them.

Ask your broker if they allow this type of listing agreement. If they don't, ask if you can offer a perpetual listing agreement with a 30-day or 60-day cancellation notice. This would require the seller to give you a written notice 30 or 60 days in advance of the expiration of the listing. The listing would carry forward until the seller gives you a cancellation notice in writing.

Handle Short Listing Requests

Many sellers feel that in order to get you motivated to sell their home, you must be in a hurry to do so. That being said, the best thing that they can think of is to ask for a short listing. Sellers, especially FSBO sellers, feel that a short listing will secure them from being "stuck" with an incompetent agent. They also feel that, since the listing is short, that you will feel a sense of urgency to sell the property. There are ways to combat this dilemma:

- *Canceled listings look bad.* When a listing gets cancelled or expires, it looks bad to buyers and to buyers' agents. Think about when you run comps for a CMA, the expired listings are a telltale sign that the property was either priced too high or something was materially wrong with it. It is important to let your sellers know this. Instead of stigmatizing their property, they should accept a longer listing duration.

- *Explain market conditions.* Whether you are taking a listing in the winter or in the heart of the spring market, there are always reasons to explain to your seller why they should give the listing the time it deserves. In the winter, of course, the market is slower and because of this you'll need more time to find buyers under these conditions. In the spring market, even though this is known as the best time to sell, there are often floods of sellers essentially doing the same thing and diluting the market, in essence making it harder to find buyers. Nonetheless, the listing needs time to ferment.

- *You need time for the ads to run.* Some real estate offices will publish ads of your listing in many periodicals. *These take time to cycle!* Tell your seller that, with all of the marketing that you will be doing for them, that you'll need time for the ads to run their course and accomplish their goal. Explain the time delays with the advertisements in the periodicals and on the websites.

- *Let the buyers have time to think about it.* Many buyers today are taking their time while shopping for a home. Some even come back to a property a month later with an offer. It is important that you don't do all of the work to procure a buyer only to have them purchase the home after the listing expires. Help your seller understand that you want to make sure that the buyers that you bring in the door are not going to buy from a future agent.

- *Short listings don't get as much advertising.* Think about it this way. If your broker knows that your listing is about to expire, they won't dump money into advertising it. It just doesn't make sense. With an extended listing duration, you can splurge in marketing their home without your broker questioning otherwise.

Summing Up

We went over a lot of material in Chapters 6 and 7. I hope you learned some new techniques that will help you with your career. If you are overwhelmed with ideas, then take a break and read these chapters again, because they contained many important topics that should not be overlooked. Calling FSBOs will seem daunting at first but you can master this art just like I did, and make a six-figure income in the process.

CHAPTER 8

The FSBO Listing Presentation

Before everything else, getting ready is the secret of success.

—HENRY FORD

FSBO Fact

Several factors appear to account for [a] decline in for-sale-by-owners: the increasing complexity of the transaction process, with more disclosures and legal requirements than ever before; the amount of time required to market and show property; and security concerns about the motivation of strangers dealing directly with owners and walking through their homes.

SOURCE: National Association of Realtors®,
Profile of Home Buyers & Sellers, 2005.

The Listing Appointment

So you finally got the listing appointment, now what? All that you have trained so hard for has now accumulated up to this final moment. You closed for the appointment over the phone, but now you must close for the listing face to face. Of all of the things you'll need at your listing appointment, your sales skills demand the greatest focus.

When you're sitting down with your sellers to close for the listing, use the same sales techniques in combination that you learned in the earlier chapters of this book.

What You'll Need

- *EVERYTHING!!!*
- Presentation portfolio
- CMA (Comparative Market Analysis)
- Resume
- Listing agreements
- Disclosures
- Calculator
- Digital camera
- Measuring tape (preferably a laser measuring device)
- Note pad
- Business cards
- Pens
- Legal pad (for taking notes)

Confirm Your Appointment

When your FSBO finally agrees to the listing appointment make sure you are prepared. Call ahead of time and confirm that you still have the appointment. Many people are hesitant to call and confirm an appointment because they're afraid that the seller might back out at the last minute. The important thing to note here is that if a seller does back out and you don't know about it, you just wasted your time, gas, and effort. Here's an effective way to confirm an appointment and ensure that the seller sticks to his or her words.

Seller: "Hello?"

Agent: "May I speak with Mr. Jones?"

S: "This is he."

A: "Mr. Jones, this is [Your Name] with [Your Company] Realty. I know that we have an appointment today at 1 P.M. I just wanted to let you know that I have done extensive research and prepared an elaborate market analysis for your home. I will see you promptly at 1 P.M."

This is very assertive. Don't ask the question, "Are we still on for today?" because if you do, you're giving the seller an option to back out. Be assertive and tell the seller that you *will* be there.

Drive by the Comps

Drive by each and every comparable that is in your CMA before you enter the sellers' home. If they know more about the comparables than you, you're in trouble. Also, don't just use the comparables that you want. Sellers know their neighborhood. They may not know the sales prices and details, but they do know what is or what was for sale in their area, so compile an accurate CMA.

Dress for Success

Does the way you look really matter? *Absolutely!* Studies show that people form a first impression the very first second they see you. There's no room for you to change their impression within that one second. Sure, you can change their impression of you after they have gotten to know you better. But why not start with a good first impression right away.

The way you dress reflects your character. If you dress like a slob, you'll be portrayed as a slob. If you dress like a professional, well . . . you'll be portrayed as a professional. Dress well for listing appointments. Don't wear a flashy suit, but wear a suit of neutral colors. If you have any awards or membership buttons, pin them on your lapel. If your intent is to provide professional service, you have to look like you mean it, wouldn't you agree? Below are some tips on ways to keep yourself from creating a negative first impression by paying some attention to the way you dress.

The Professional Fashion

- *Wear solid dark color suits.* By solid, I mean no patterns or loud pin-striped suits. Solid black, blue, or brown suits are professional colors to wear to an appointment. Try to make it a two-piece suit or a blazer with coordinating dress pants. For women, suits are very popular these days, and you can follow these same guidelines. If you choose to wear a skirt, keep it neutral and professional. Avoid anything that may be flashy or revealing.

- *Coordinate your suit with your shirt.* Wear a long-sleeve button-front shirt that matches your outerwear. A V-neck sweater is a great professional look for winter, which can be worn over your dress shirt.

- *Wear a neutral tie.* There are so many tie patterns out there, yet so many of them are bad. A tie with a neutral color and a very simple pattern will suffice.

- *Wear dress shoes.* Many people will only look at a person's shoes to reach an impression. Wear shoes that are up to class with your outfit.

- *Have a clean-cut look.* For men, keep your face clean and professional. Long hair and beards are okay, but they may cost you some listings. It's best to keep your hair short and your facial hair to a minimum.

  For women, if you wear your hair long down your back, it may be time to think about a new style. Looking professional is very important for business pictures and first impressions. Work on a look that you can keep. That way, your pictures will still look like you as time goes on.

- *Go easy on the cologne/perfume.* It's good to smell nice at appointments, as long as you know your limit. Overpowering yourself with cologne or perfume will only draw attention away from your presentation and keep attention focused on your scent.

- *Limit your jewelry.* If you're a jewelry person, leave the excess at home. A professional should wear only one ring. For women, keep it simple. One necklace and a pair of simple earrings is more than enough to keep your look professional.

The Comparative Market Analysis

Never go to a listing appointment without at least a preliminary Comparative Market Analysis (CMA) prepared. When I say a preliminary CMA, this means that you haven't seen the property, and the only information you have is what was given to you over the phone or what you received from the FSBO ad. Every CMA should include sold, active, and expired listings. What expired listings tell us is that those homes didn't sell because they were overpriced.

Be Punctual

Arrive to your listing appointment a few minutes early. It's always better to be early than late. Even better, arrive ten minutes early and drive around the neighborhood until your appointment is ready. In the meantime get a feel for the neighborhood or search for nearby FSBOs and find out what they're asking. By doing this, you'll show that you're well prepared and in tune with the neighborhood market.

Tour the Home

One of the first things you do when you arrive at your appointment is take a tour of the seller's home. See this as an opportunity to build rapport with the sellers.

Five Tips for Building Rapport While Touring the Home

1. *Find something in common.* The best way to build rapport is to find the common denominators. This could be hobbies, sports, interests, or personal tastes. While touring the home look for signs of common denominators. For example, if you like antiques and you find the seller has a considerable number of them, strike up a conversation about antiques on a personal, non-business level to help the seller unwind and become comfortable with you.

2. *Show off your knowledge.* Show that you know the terminology and history of specific home features. For example, if you know the name of the style that the granite counters are made of, show them that you know. If you know the history of specific features in the home, *tell them.* Show off your knowledge as long as you're not telling them something that is obvious or redundant.

3. *Give compliments.* Tastefully compliment the seller where appropriate. When you find features of a home that you sincerely admire, give a compliment. For example, you can say, "I love how

you coordinated the colors of your kitchen. It really keeps your eyes moving." Be as unique and creative as you can be. Try to avoid boring compliments like, "This house is really nice," or "I like your furniture." Compliments can go a long way if you can say them like you mean them.

4. *Ask questions of concern.* If you have any concerns about the home, bring them up to the seller. For example, if you stumble on a room that can use some painting, ask the seller whether they plan on painting it. You can say it like this: "A fresh coat of paint would certainly make this room look sharp. *Do you plan on painting it?*" Addressing these questions shows that you are looking out for the seller's interest.

5. *Point out the good selling features.* Look for valuable selling features in the home. You will use these to highlight the home. These can also be used for building rapport. Sellers love to hear about the positive amenities. Point out the positive features to get on a good footing with the seller prior to the listing presentation.

The Presentation Setting

When the time comes to sit down and give your presentation, remember that where you sit and how you act are critical to your presentation.

Be the Center of Attention

Suggest that you sit at the kitchen table. The kitchen has more significance for decision making than any other room in the house. More importantly, coordinate the seating arrangements of the table to your advantage. If you want to take charge, you have to be sure that the sellers can't exchange body language under your nose. Have the sellers sit next to each other and you sit on the opposite side of the table. This keeps their focus on you and not each other. When they are able to exchange body language with one another it takes away from your control of the situation.

Body Language

Your body can communicate in volume to your seller even if you are unaware of it. Control your own body language, but also pay attention to the body language of the sellers. Here are some tips:

- *Make eye contact.* Eye contact is very important for controlling a conversation. Be sure to make eye contact with your prospects during your presentation.

- *Smile.* Smiling shows that you are comfortable and confident. Smile when you feel it's necessary, and make sure your sellers are smiling back. If they aren't smiling back, there may be some barriers or issues that need to be addressed. Use this as a means to probe for underlying concerns your sellers may have.

- *Keep your hands free.* What you do with your hands and arms must give the proper impression to your prospect. Don't fold your arms. This is a common negative posture. Although it can mean many different things to different sellers, the point here is, don't do it. Keep your arms open or at your side. Better yet, hold something. For example, if you hold a note pad, it can indicate that you are ready to work and that you came prepared.

- *Lean in.* While your sellers speak, lean forward. This will show that you are interested in what they are talking about. And when you speak, also lean forward. It gets their attention and keeps them listening to what you have to say.

- *Sit still.* If you find yourself fidgeting with your fingers, hands, or feet, *stop*. Although this can indicate that you are anxious, many people will take it as a sign of boredom. This can be very distracting to others. Even though you may not even know you are doing it, your seller may be focused on your tapping fingers and not on your presentation. Try to remain calm and comfortable and get the sellers' undivided attention.

The Presentation

Now you are ready to make your presentation, a key element of which is your presentation portfolio.

The Presentation Portfolio

The purpose of a visual aid is to capture the attention of your audience through visual stimulation. Combining your verbal presentation with visual aids makes for a powerful listing presentation.

For good presentation materials visit an office supply store. I recommend a tent-style presentation booklet, as shown in Figure 8-1. This style of portfolio is effective because it is easy to use and also keeps the sellers from looking down at the table.

Figure 8-1. Presentation booklet.

You can also use a laptop for your presentations. A notebook computer will show that you are in tune with technology. It will also pull your prospects into the presentation, especially if you use interactive features. You can use Microsoft PowerPoint or similar programs to give your presentation a "wow" factor.

You'll be surprised by the number of agents that don't use a portfolio. Many feel that they are so good that they don't need one. This couldn't be further from the truth. Portfolios organize your offer in a manner that the prospect can understand and *remember*. Portfolios should not be an option, but a must-have.

Four Sections of Your Portfolio Layout

- Your Company
- You
- Your Offer
- The Investment (Benefit)

1. *Your Company.* The first section of your portfolio should be about your company. Have all of your office awards, if any, that your company received. Your office mission statement should also be briefly mentioned. Do not clutter the presentation with too many words. Keep it simple and concise.

2. *You.* The second section should be about you. Mention your accomplishments, your level of education, and your mission statement. (I will cover how to create your mission statement in Chapter

10.) In this section of your presentation, mention what homes you have sold in the area, if any, and how many homes your office has sold in that specific area. Also include what experience you have in the area such as community and volunteer work, or whether you ever resided in the area. You should have no more than three pages about yourself.

3. *Your Offer.* In the third section you'll want to start with what you and your company offer the sellers in terms of marketing. Include sample newspaper ads, flyers, and brochures of listings that your office has published. It is very important to talk about what you offer over the competition. Also include a page about what you personally offer, such as holding open houses, offering personalized service, a custom name rider on your "For Sale" sign, etc.

4. *The Investment.* To sum up your listing presentation, you'll need to mention the brokerage fee. Notice how I say *brokerage fee* and not commission. Throughout the entire presentation, the brokerage fee will be in the front of their mind. So how do you convince sellers that your brokerage fee is fair and worth every penny of what you're asking? This is a significant task. I'll dive into the justification tips and suggested dialogue later in this chapter.

Don't Count Your Income Early

Enter your listing appointment without the expectations of getting the listing. If you go to a listing appointment with money on your mind you will be out of touch with what your real goal should be: to offer quality and professional service to the seller. Also keep in mind that thinking about the brokerage fee will influence your thought process, and the seller will know what's on your mind. You'll know when you're operating at your highest potential when you can't find the time to count your income.

Explain the Brokerage Fee

When you bring up the brokerage fee to the seller, be certain they know what the brokerage fee includes. Stay true to the average brokerage fee for the area of your listing. Mention that you offer the co-op broker whatever the average is for the area. For example, if you were to tell the seller that the brokerage fee would be 5 percent, also let them know that you are giving the other broker (the co-op) 2.5 percent. Point out that when many agents give lower than average quotes, they usually cut the co-op brokerage fee to compensate for their loss. This ultimately leads to fewer showings and risks the property not selling.

Leave Them with Something

Always leave something with the sellers if you have to leave without getting the listing. By "something" I mean a folder with all of your information inside, including your resume, the preliminary CMA, a list of homes you or your office sold in the area, and your business card. This will keep you on their table and in their mind. You can have custom folders printed with your information on them. This is a professional touch and says a lot about you.

Pricing the Listing

You must try your hardest to list the property at market value the very day you get the listing, not two weeks or a month later. Many sellers want to start off higher than the property is worth and then come down later. You must stress that this is a huge mistake. When you initially go into the market too high, you will miss all of the buyers that are in the price range that you ultimately will come down to. When you finally reduce the price those buyers will have already found a property or will think your listing is stale due to excessive market time accrued. Not only that, but the offers you do get will start low because they will perceive the seller as "desperate" due to the market time and price reductions.

Why Most FSBOs Are Overpriced

- FSBOs don't have tools to accurately appraise their own home at market value.
- FSBOs, from the start, try to "test" the market at a higher price.
- Many FSBOs include the brokerage fee in the already high price.
- Some sellers are not in a hurry to sell and are willing

to stay on the market for an extremely long period of time without selling.

When you think about it, FSBOs don't have access to the tools to accurately price and market their property themselves. And most sellers choose to sell FSBO because they want to save on the brokerage fee. At the same time, they build that into the price of the home. But not *all* FSBOs are overpriced.

Dealing with Overpriced FSBOs

It seems that FSBOs not only want to save on the commission but they also end up overpricing the property. When negotiating the listing price with the sellers, it seems many will try to keep an already high price to absorb the commission they must pay. This brings us to a common dilemma: If they don't believe the problem, they won't believe the solution. It is your job to educate and inform the sellers, but it is the seller's job to pick an agent whom they trust to give them the best advice on pricing the property.

Sometimes the FSBOs still stick to their price even after you've hammered and drilled the facts and statistics of how they benefit by pricing it at the market value. When this happens you have two choices:

1. You can take the listing but get the sellers to agree that they will reduce the price at a predetermined date—say, after one month—if the buyer turnout is lackluster. If the sellers don't reduce the price now nor agree to the predetermined price reduc-

tion, then you have to make a decision. If you feel that the seller may come down in price eventually, then you can give a shot at listing it, as long as you have the time to sit on an overpriced turkey.

2. Your second option is to refer the listing to another agent and let them waste their time. Then you can try to be the rebound agent after the property doesn't sell with the other agent. Work it out with that agent so that when the property doesn't sell they refer you to get the rebound. In this situation, odds are that as the second or third agent you will have a better chance at selling the listing. Once the seller realizes that it's not the agent's fault and comes to terms with reality, you should be able to lower the price.

My advice is to take the listing with the understanding that you'll reduce the price at a predetermined date. Here's what you do: When you're sitting down with your seller at the listing presentation, pull out a price change form and pre-date it for the date on which you both agree to reduce the price. Have the seller initial the paperwork right there. Now you'll have a shot to market the property at market value if the property doesn't sell by that predetermined date.

When to Take Overpriced Listings

If you take the overpriced listing, you might just sell it if the right buyer comes along with more money to spend.

For example, you might find a buyer who has an elderly parent living in the neighborhood, and who is willing to pay a premium for that location. Not only that, but there's a good chance that you'll get good buyer leads from your sign calls in front of the listing. If you don't have many listings or none at all, even an overpriced listing gives you the ammunition to list other properties and work with buyer leads.

Simply having some listings in your inventory can give you an upper hand at listing appointments, especially when you mention that you are selling a home in the seller's area. Not to mention, holding open houses can open new doors that you didn't otherwise have access to. Many sellers find it hard to list with an agent who doesn't have any listings in their inventory. So if you don't have anything going for you, take the overpriced listing and use it as leverage for acquiring more listings.

LIST, LIST, LIST!!!

Listings are the name of the game. You can build a listing inventory that sells itself. Why work with a buyer here and a buyer there when you can be selling multiple listings at once and increase your sales dramatically. I'm not saying that you shouldn't work with buyers. If you have serious buyers that need a home, by all means, find them a home. What I *am* saying is that if you look at the big picture, you can leverage your time by focusing on listings, sell more properties by focusing on listings, and multiply your business exponentially by focusing on listings. You can't do that by focusing on buyers. There is more money to be made listing homes than selling homes, so just make sure you know where you want to put most of your effort in order to maximize your returns.

Track Your Progress

Keep yourself on track with your goals. Follow your progress with a chart that graphs your listings over the months. Here's what you do. Organize a chart for the year. On the bottom of the chart (X-axis) label the twelve months ahead. On the left side of the chart (Y-axis) have the quantity of listings for the months (see a sample chart in Figure 8-2).

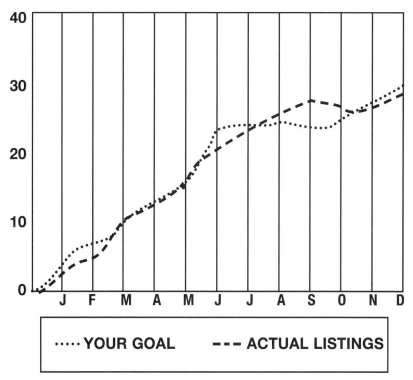

Figure 8-2. Tracking your goals.

At the beginning of each month, draw a line for your projected listing goal for the month (black line). At the end of the month, add a line showing your actual listings (gray line). As the months go by you will be able to see how your actual number of listings stack up against your goals. This will give you a track record for your month-by-month production and, over time, your year-by-year production, compared with your goals.

If you want to go a step further, add two lines to the chart to track your monthly closings and your advertising budget. Put the dollar amounts on the left side (Y-axis) to keep a record of your budget. This will help you monitor your expenses and sales over the months.

CHAPTER 9

The Marketing Plan

I keep marketing for the same reason a pilot keeps his engines running once he gets off the ground.

—WILLIAM WRIGLEY JR., FOUNDER, WRIGLEY COMPANY

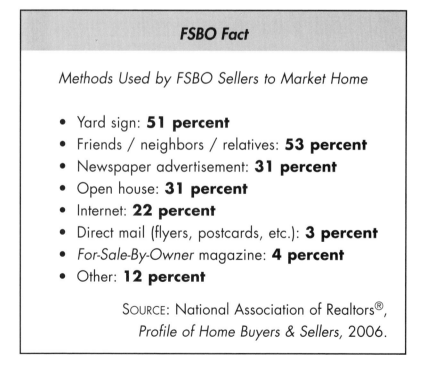

FSBO Fact

Methods Used by FSBO Sellers to Market Home

- Yard sign: **51 percent**
- Friends / neighbors / relatives: **53 percent**
- Newspaper advertisement: **31 percent**
- Open house: **31 percent**
- Internet: **22 percent**
- Direct mail (flyers, postcards, etc.): **3 percent**
- *For-Sale-By-Owner* magazine: **4 percent**
- Other: **12 percent**

SOURCE: National Association of Realtors®,
Profile of Home Buyers & Sellers, 2006.

Market Exposure

Throughout this book we've discussed ways to help sculpt yourself into a successful FSBO listing and selling machine. In this chapter we'll focus on ways to get your name out in front of as many people as possible within your financial reach. There are many ways you can market yourself. Creative ideas will distinguish your marketing from the competition. You don't want to waste money on pointless advertising that won't be recognized. Do what works best.

I'm sure you can find many marketing magazines that are targeted specifically at real estate agents or even your office brand name. For references to marketing resources, refer to Appendix A in the back of the book.

Six Great Marketing Ideas

1. *Car Magnets.* Have car magnets made. It's rather inexpensive and shows professionalism when arriving to an appointment. Of course you wouldn't want to put car magnets on a rust bucket car. If that's the case, wait until you have a decent car to put them on. With car magnets you may get prospects to walk up to your car and pick your brain with questions about the neighborhood and the activity. I've experienced this many times myself. These are good leads to follow up on. People who ask questions are doing so for a reason: They are getting ready to make a move. A number of

times, when stopped at a red light, I've had people ask for my business card after seeing my car magnets.

Magnets aren't disposable advertising; they will last you a long time. And, now that I think of it, they cost about as much as a single monthly farm mailer, but they will outlast and out-lead a monthly mailer. Have your phone number printed very large on the magnet. Many times people will be looking from a distance, so make sure everyone can see your contact name and phone number. Refer to Appendix A for resources on car magnet printer companies.

2. *Flyers.* Flyers are not as effective as letters, but with flyers you can canvas a larger area for less money. Flyers should never be sent to your farm for reasons we'll discuss in Chapter 10. An effective flyer should be to the point and present an offer of some kind. Make the flyers double-sided and printed on bright, eye-catching card stock. If you can afford to print in color and use a higher quality printer, by all means do it. If neither you nor your brokerage firm have a high quality printer, then a regular copy machine is all you need.

Sadly, the vast majority of people who receive your flyer will throw them into the trash without even looking at them. But all you need is one lead to make this effort worthwhile. Dollar for dollar, marketing with flyers will pay off. It may not be on the first mailing or the second. But if you are persistent you will see results. You'll want to keep flyers in your car at all times. Leave them wherever you go: grocery stores, gas stations, convenience stores, and restaurants.

3. *Over-the-Phone CMAs.* Offer a free, no-obligation, over-the-phone CMA in your advertisements. This is a great way to get sellers to call you. Every real estate agent offers a free CMA. Now you can offer the same thing—but over the phone. How easy is that? You can put this on your flyers, stationary, and website. Because you can't see the inside of the seller's home over the phone, give them a price range of the market value of their home. Tell them that in order for you to give a more precise figure you'll have to see the inside of their home in person. Then, while at their home, you close for the listing.

4. *Personal Website.* Technology makes it easier for us to reach people than ever before. Internet exposure is one easy and effective way to generate quality leads. More and more, buyers and sellers are using their computers to research ways to buy or sell a home. But the Internet has spoiled consumers. They want to know everything instantly. If a seller or buyer can interview you virtually over the Internet through your website, you can essentially let your website go to work for you.

It's like having a virtual assistant. Creating a website for yourself will be a marketing investment that can reap huge returns over the long run. In addition, you can use your web address in every aspect of your marketing.

There are many website builders that offer services specifically for real estate agents. Also, check with your brokerage firm. Many real estate companies offer website services designed for their company and have templates for use by their agents. This can be beneficial if you want to have an MLS search option on your site.

Also, this can be an excellent way to bring in buyers. You can encourage buyers and sellers to visit your website and be sure to mention your "free" MLS search engine option. When prospects sign up to use your MLS search engine, you can follow up with them and convert them into sales. You can acquire quality leads in your sleep!

When creating a website, try to buy a domain name that is easy to think of and remember, such as your first and last name dot com. If your name is already taken as a domain name, you can make up a short slogan with your name in it such as www.realtorjim.com, or something catchy like www.sellyourhomewithjoan.com. You can create a simple 8- to 10-page website for around $500, if you shop around. If you have the funds, it's a good idea to spend a little more to create something a bit more catchy and interactive. For more details on how to make a powerful website, and for great website builder resources, check out Appendix A under Agent Website Builder Services. If you're new, just get your name on the Internet with a basic website so you can use your website address on your business cards, For-Sale signs, magnets, and stationary.

5. *Business Cards.* Another very important marketing tool is business cards. Your business card in many instances will be the only thing that a prospect has to judge you by. With that in mind, make your business cards look professional. If you work for a big company, there are businesses that specialize in printing your cards with your specific office logos and award icons. You should contact your broker before buying any business cards to see if they offer these advantages. If you don't work for a big company try to make your card look as professional as possible. Avoid bright, flashy colors when designing your business card. You don't want to come off as loud. A professional-looking card should be what to shoot for.

Have your face on the card! It doesn't matter what you look like. People will always feel more comfortable with the person whose picture they have seen.

While you're ordering your business cards, you can also purchase business card magnets. These will go into the FSBO mailing packages you send out right after talking with prospects. The idea is to get the seller to put your magnetic business card on their refrigerator. Your magnet will stay there until the house goes up for sale. Additionally, these magnets don't expire like magnetic calendars do.

6. *Name Riders.* Another key to marketing your name is to buy rider signs that contain your name, cell phone number, and, if you have one, your website address. By the way, if you don't already own a cell phone, you'll definitely need to buy one. You can't run an efficient real estate career without one.

Name rider signs will hang directly underneath your For-Sale sign post in the front of your listing. This will connect you directly to the buyer. How nice is it when a buyer calls you on your listing and actually buys it? Now that would be an investment that can reap some major returns. Also, other homeowners in the neighborhood will get used to seeing your name. Conveniently, if they choose to call you, your phone number is right next to your name. If your office requires you to make your own For-Sale signs, have the sign made with your name, phone number, and web address already on the sign itself, so you can avoid making additional name riders.

You can also try to get your photo on the rider

sign. It may be difficult to find a company that's able to print your photo on a rider sign, so do it yourself. An easy solution is to have a printer shop make *magnetic* decals of your photo. Or you can have *adhesive* decals of your photo made, which may be less expensive and are also more permanent. Pick the one that is best for you. Refer to Appendix A for resources to purchase name rider signs online.

Having More to Offer Than the Competition

I've had many listing appointments where I was in direct competition with some of the real estate industry leaders in the area. And with my experience of only one year in this business, you can imagine how hard it was to come out the champion. Well, I beat the competition in virtually every challenge that I was faced with. I even beat the *top* producing agent in the area at the time. If you're wondering how I did it, I wouldn't be able to tell you exactly because success in such a competitive endeavor is not a science, it's an art. And, as an art, every listing appointment should paint a different picture. What I *can* teach you, however, is everything that helped me to paint these successful pictures.

The Bottom Line

The majority of the sellers you will face will be looking for these qualities in an agent:

1. Honesty
2. Experience
3. Professionalism
4. Aggressiveness

If you show that you have the energy, ambition, confidence, and the right marketing tools to your advantage, and you present this to your seller in an honest fashion, you'll have a leg-up on the competition. The bottom line, however, would be your answers to the seller's basic questions: What do you offer? How does it help me? And how much is it? It's important to be honest when answering these questions. Your honesty will significantly increase their comfort level with you.

What Do You Offer?

Offer a guarantee! If you can guarantee that the newspaper ads will be run or web ads will be placed, then tell them that. Sellers like guarantees and are smart enough to steer away from a sales pitch. Guarantee an open house every weekend, or every other weekend, or as long as there are buyers coming through the door. If you can't sit the open house yourself, then have an assistant do it for you. And if you're clever, you'll have new agents sit your open house and avoid paying an assistant. Just convince the agents that they can get buyer leads and possibly sell the house by taking three hours out of their day to sit an open house. What would they have to lose?

How Does It Help Me?

For each agent and their respective office, the answer to this question will vary slightly. The best way to tackle this question is to go over what you offer one by one and explain the answers to each. For example, if you offer more newspaper ads than the competition, tell the seller that they'll have more market exposure and increase their odds of selling. If you offer a home warranty, get the statistics from the warranty provider and tell the seller that their home will have a faster sale, a better chance of selling, and sell for a higher price. And cite the statistics from the home warranty provider that you use.

Ultimately you are offering yourself. Your professional service and your aggressive sales approach will be your offer to the seller. How does that help them?

You have to admit, in this business sellers have many agents to choose from. What may be different about you is that you are a full-time agent (I hope), you are ambitious, and you are in tune with today's market. If the seller asks you the question, "You've only been doing this for how long?" (and let's say you're new), then you can say something like this: "Many agents who have been in this business for several years or more don't have the enterprising drive that I possess. Many of them are content with a listing every couple of months and are bitter about servicing them." Although this is true, I don't mean that all experienced agents fit this character. What I mean is that across the spectrum of experienced agents you'll always find agents that fit these characteristics. What I'm getting at is that you are not one of them, and you can state that as your advantage.

How Much Is It?

How much do you charge? You should already know how much you charge. But how do you convince a seller that you're worth what you're asking? That's why we discuss the price of your services at the end of the presentation. You should have enough to offer them to justify what you're asking for your brokerage fee. Keep in mind that intangible characteristics also count, such as your character, experience, honesty, or aggressiveness. These are valuable assets, so be sure to put weight on the intangibles you possess.

Your Resume

Every time you are face to face (or ear to ear) with a potential prospect you are essentially in a job interview. The seller is your employer and you are the employee. Employers (sellers) interview many employment applicants (agents) for the job but will only settle for the one who sets him- or herself apart from the rest. Your resume should do exactly that. It should tell your seller how much experience you have, any awards you have, and what exactly you can offer them if you were to take on the job. A resume should be concise but pack a punch. You can use a Microsoft Word resume template to give you some help with your layout. A sample resume is included in Appendix C.

Keep copies of your resume in your car, and make sure that every envelope you mail has one in it. You can print these on fancy linen paper and really give it a professional quality. If you print on linen paper, try to use a laser printer. Inkjet printers tend to smudge easily on this type of paper. Also, keep resumes in the listing presentation folder that you leave with your new or potential clients. You don't want to leave anything out.

E-Mail Drip-Marketing

As I discussed in Chapter 5, The FSBO System, you can use FSBO e-mail addresses to create a unique marketing system. Obtain e-mail addresses from FSBO lead provider services, websites such as craigslist.com, other sites that specialize in homes for sale by owner, or even from prospects who register on your personal website. Compile these e-mail addresses and advertise to them through a drip-marketing service.

E-mail drip-marketing is an automated e-mail campaign that sends out a series of ads to prospects of your choice or to prospects that choose to sign up for this service through your website. Here's how it works. Organize an e-mail campaign structure that sends a series of e-mail advertisements in seven-day intervals. It can start off with an introduction, then go into a problem-solution ad, and then give information about how to handle the transaction, etc. To get a better idea of the topics and structure of e-mail drip campaigns, here is an example.

Week 1:   *Introduction:* Introduce yourself to the prospect.

Week 2:   *Problem-Solution:* Acknowledge the problem, offer your solution.

Week 3:   *Staging the Home for Showings:* Give away information to show off your skill level.

Week 4:   *Understanding the Paperwork:* Demonstrate the overwhelming paperwork involved in a transaction.

Week 5:   *Information on Qualifying Buyers:* Show how to work with loan officers to get buyers approved for a loan.

Week 6:   *Benefits of Using an Agent:* Describe the benefits and financial advantages of using a professional.

Week 7:   *The Offer Contract:* Explain the offer contract and how to select a real estate attorney.

Week 8:   *Inspection Issues:* Describe how inspections can make or break the transaction.

Week 9:   *Dealing with the Closing:* Explain what is required at closing and what to look out for.

All you have to do is set up the prospects' e-mail in the system, and then sit back and let it do its job. The system will send weekly e-mails to your prospects without you even being there. One great feature that many of these systems offer is that you can monitor when prospects opened the e-mail and what links they clicked on. If your prospects decide to opt out of the e-mail campaign, they have the option to do so. Also, the system notifies you when you get new prospects that sign up for this service through your website. Here are two suggested resources to get you started:

www.intersend.com
www.proautoresponder.com

Direct Mail

Right after you get a listing, *tell the world!* Make direct-mail flyers that advertise "Just Listed in Your Neighborhood." Mail them to the surrounding area of your new listing. Once you have listings you'll notice that it's easier to acquire even more listings because sellers want to list with someone who has experience, and listings are proof of that.

Do you have any special offers? Some agents offer a $500 or $1,000 credit to the seller at closing for using them as their agent (which is usually split between you and your broker, so get your broker's permission first before you print the offer). A free market analysis is also a very common offer. Even better, as we previously mentioned, is an over-the-phone CMA. Include your offer on all stationery that you create. You can also offer free virtual tours, or a free home warranty. Whatever it is that you choose, just make sure that your offer is visible on your flyer, or the flyer is guaranteed to end up in the garbage can.

Keep a stack of these flyers in your car at all times and leave them wherever you go. Leave your mark in the form of your advertisements. When you add up all of these tips, it increases your odds of listing and selling more homes.

Written Testimonials

The best way to convince FSBOs to list with you is to prove that other sellers have put their trust in you and were satisfied. After every transaction that you close, create a written testimonial that the seller can sign for you. Here is a sample of such a testimonial:

I had my home on the market by owner for five months asking $300k and had no luck. Then, [Your Name] listed it for $300k and we had multiple offers in just two weeks. I wish I used [Your Name's] professional service from the start.

Be creative and as specific as possible when writing your testimonials. Don't exaggerate or you won't get your seller's endorsement.

Keep a page in your presentation portfolio devoted to your written testimonials. People feel more comfortable buying a good or service from a person if someone else already has, especially if the person who experienced it praises it. This is just common sense. It's like applying for a job and having the new employer call your old bosses to see how well you performed. When your new employer (your potential client) sees that others benefited from your service, they'll have plenty reason to hire you. You can even incorporate these testimonials into your farm mailings (we'll get into farming in Chapter 10).

Use testimonials in your advertisements and in your presentation. Here's an idea: When you close a transaction, have someone take your picture with the satisfied sellers. Use these pictures as testimonials in your FSBO advertising. A great way to sway FSBOs onto your side is to show that many other FSBOs experienced great success through you.

CHAPTER 10

Farming for FSBOs

Failure is the path of least persistence.

—Unknown Author

FSBO Fact

Seventy-one percent of sellers said they used an agent from a previous transaction, or took a recommendation from friends, neighbors, or family, who were pleased with their agent.

Source: National Association of Realtors®, *Profile of Home Buyers and Sellers*, 2005.

Now let's get into working your farm. A *farm* is an area that you strategically designate to send your monthly mailing advertisements to. When you mail to your farm every month, over time the seeds will blossom into a profitable listing bank. First, plant the seeds, then, reap the harvest. The long-term goal is to rely on referrals as your main source of income, not FSBOs. Little by little as you sell listings, dump more and more money into your farm and referral business. The industry pros suggest devoting 10 percent of your income to marketing and farming. This will pay off in the long run, with less work demanded from you to be at top production.

Finding the Most Profitable Farm

Whether you have already picked your farm area or you're still in the process of getting started, you should make sure that it's a profitable farm before you sink money into it every month. Any farm is a good farm, but some farms are better than others, and you'll want the best bang for your buck. There are a few key elements to a farm from which you might find important:

1. *Turnover Rate of Homes in the Neighborhood.* Some neighborhoods turn over more slowly than others. When you have some neighborhoods in mind, go onto the MLS and look at the number of homes that have sold in those areas in the past year. Also look at the market time of those homes that have sold. Of course, the faster the turnover rate the better. The average family moves once every three to five years. So do the math on your farm. If you have a farm of 500 homes and, on average, homes sell every three to five years, it means that between 100 and 166 homes will be turning over per year on average. Eventually, even

if you list only 20 percent of the homes that turn over in that farm, you'll get between twenty to thirty-three listings per year!

2. *The Size of Your Farm.* Determine how many households you will be mailing to in your farm. The larger your farm is, the better, if you can afford it. If you *can't* afford it, try starting out with a farm of 200 to 300 homes. The optimum farm would be about 1,000 homes. Remember, this is a numbers game. The more people get to know you, the more leads and listings you'll get.

3. *Type of Homes.* If you live in a city where the neighborhoods have their own unique housing stock, this could be something to take advantage of. For example, in Chicago many of the neighborhoods have their own predominant housing stock, such as brick bungalows or English-style homes. This is a great opportunity to target that niche of owners. You can mail the sellers information and news about their specific style of property. Better yet, you can be a specialist for certain property types. This will give you an upper hand over the competition at your listing appointments.

4. *Median Market Price.* Usually, a neighborhood's median market price is correlated to the turnover rate of homes in that area (to a degree). This means that, typically, the lower turnover rates are found in high-class neighborhoods, and higher

turnover rates are found in mid- to low-class neighborhoods. If you're thinking about farming in a high-class neighborhood, where the homes' median market price is significantly above the rest of the market, you may want to examine the turnover rate of that neighborhood. Chances are they don't move too often. The ideal areas are middle-class neighborhoods, which have a great turnover rate and an attractive median sales price—which I find is the best of both worlds.

5. *Your Competition.* Do your homework on competition in the area that you're considering to claim as your farm. You don't want too much competition in your farm area or you'll be losing some ground to them. If you live in the area that you are considering to market as your farm, check your mail to see how many competitive farm mailings you receive. Sometimes you may get an advertisement flyer from an agent but never see anything from them again. This is typical. This wouldn't be considered competition. Those are the agents that start well but then give up early, as we discussed in Chapter 2. But do keep an eye on the agents who mail your neighborhood every month. If there are a few of them mailing consistently, you may want to reconsider your decision to claim that neighborhood as your farm. Ideally, having little to no competition is the best scenario.

Tracking Your Farm

Print out a map of your farm area, preferably a plat map or an aerial view map. You can even draw the map yourself, as shown in Figure 10-1. When you get a listing in your farm, stick a green tack pin on your listings, stick a red tack pin on all of the FSBOs in your farm area and, lastly, to keep track of the competition's production in your farm, stick a black pin in all of your competitor's listings.

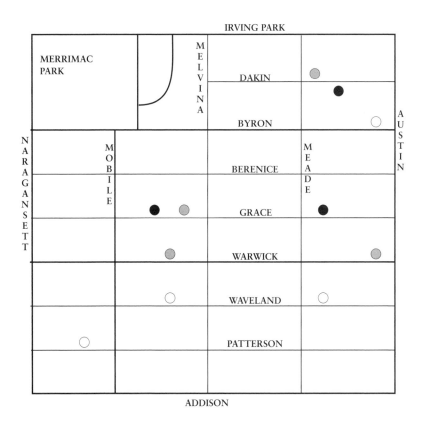

Figure 10-1. Mapping your farm area.

Automating Your Farm Mailing System

A bulk-mail permit allows you to mail large quantities in similar zip codes for less than the retail stamp rate. Additionally, these permits make the job of mass mailing much easier. If your office doesn't have a bulk-mail permit, talk to your broker about buying a permit for everyone in the office to share. This will save you the trouble and money of doing it yourself. Once you have a permit, all you have to do is buy an ink stamp with your permit number on it and you'll never have to lick another stamp for your farm mailings again. For additional information about a bulk-mail permit, or how to acquire one, contact your local post office.

Five Tips for Effective Automated Mailings

1. *Have someone else do your dirty work.* Time is money. If you can save time (money) by having someone else do your tedious tasks, by all means go for it. Contact a few print shops to see whether one of them will print, label, and stuff all of your envelopes for you every month. You should be able to find a printer willing to take on the task of printing the envelope letterhead, printing the letter, stuffing the envelope, and addressing the envelope. Then all you will have to do is pick up the batch every month and take it to the post office for bulk-mail delivery. This may sound complicated to organize, but it is much less complicated than doing all of the work yourself. Put your time

to better use than stuffing, licking, and addressing envelopes two days out of every month.

2. *Customize your envelope.* You can create a slogan (which we'll cover in more detail later in the chapter) and print that along with your address on the envelope. The printer should also pre-print the post office permit stamp on the postage side of the envelope, as shown in Figure 10-2. Try to set it up so you can keep most of your envelopes at the print shop; then e-mail the shop your monthly newsletter for them to run off, stuff, and address.

Figure 10-2. Sample of preprinted permit stamp.

3. *Give homeowners a reason to open your mail.* If you are typing a newsletter with valuable information, or if you have a gift inside the envelope, such as a yearly calendar, make them find it. As shown above in Figure 10-2, if you print on your envelope, "FREE GIFT INSIDE!" or "WHAT'S HAPPENING IN YOUR NEIGHBORHOOD?"

more of your sellers are likely to open the letters out of curiosity. It's an easy addition to your farm mailer, and it's very effective.

4. *Personalize your newsletters.* If your printer creates your letters with a laser printer, add a personal touch to your monthly letters. At the bottom of your letter include a picture of your signature. How is this done, you ask? Well, you can scan your signature into your computer, and paste it as a picture on your newsletters. That way if you print your farm mailers with a laser printer, it will look like you signed each newsletter by hand. I know this is not as personal as you would wish, but couldn't your time be put to better use than signing 500 to 1,000 letters? I thought so.

5. *Create your farm mailing labels.* By the way, if you are wondering how to acquire your mailing address labels, ask your broker. Your office should have a program that creates the labels for you; all you do is type in the address coordinates and the street names for which you would like labels. The labels are then printed out on address stickers. This program can also be purchased by agents for personal use.

Keep Mailing!

Please note that I said *monthly* mailing. Most agents start farming but end up abandoning their farm or spreading the mailings too far apart to be effective. The reason most agents fail to consistently mail to their farm every month is because it costs money and they expect a quick response to their mailing. A quick response does not happen. What *does* happen is that over time, you'll be the first person in a seller's mind when it comes time to sell. Farming is not for the impatient. It may take one or two years for you to see the sought-after results of farming. But once you get into the habit of mailing your farm every single month, there is a way that your farm area can reap a far richer harvest than other agents have. I discuss this below in the Farm FSBOs section.

There are books available that offer pre-written letter templates for real estate agents. If you aren't a good writer, such a book is a good investment. All you'll need to do is type in your name at the top and you have a newsletter. There are also companies that will print advertisements on virtually anything that you can think of. Take advantage of your creativity and make yourself stand apart from the rest with different marketing ideas.

Whatever it is that you decide to mail, just make sure that your budget allows you to continue your mailings consistently every single month.

Farm FSBOs

The FSBO leads with the best chance of listing will be ones found in your farm. Think about it this way: If there's a FSBO in your farm area to whom you have regularly sent your monthly mailings, who would have a better chance of getting the listing, you, or the competition the seller has never heard of? The answer is easy . . . *you would!* I can't recall how many FSBOs I listed that were from my farm area. This is a technique that you can use to speed up the results of your farm harvest. Once sellers start to see your signs popping up in their neighborhood and, on top of that, start receiving your monthly mailings, you can be sure that they'll be considering you to list their home when they decide to sell.

Farm Fuel

When you get a listing in your farm, use that for material in your monthly mailings. You can advertise, "Just Listed in Your Area" or "Another Home Listed by [Your name]." If you don't have any listings or sales in your farm area, use your office's listings. I would advise not to mail flyers to your farm. Flyers should be sent to areas outside of your farm. You'll want the people in your farm to get to know you. You can't do that with a flyer. I suggest typing a unique farm newsletter every month. Focus your letter on their specific neighborhood. For example, you can write letters about what's new in the local real estate market.

Your Mug Shot

Like I said earlier in the book, it doesn't matter what you look like, *just have your picture taken.* Wedding pictures and college graduation photos just don't cut it. Have your photo taken by a professional photographer, *not* at a local grocery chain store. Those photos are used for passports, not real estate agents. Make sure it's a photo that looks like you and is from a real photographer. It may cost a bit more but it will be worth it in the long run.

Your Slogan

Think long and hard about this one. Your slogan will be used in all of your advertising from the time you create it until the time you retire from real estate (hopefully, that's a long time from now). Your slogan should be short but powerful. It doesn't necessarily have to rhyme with your name, like in this example: "Howard Gold—Everything I touch turns to *SOLD*." Although tying in your full name with your slogan is a good idea, you can also explore other options for slogans that only use one part of your name.

I decided to go with a slogan that builds my character, since I am younger than the average agent in the industry. My slogan is: "John Maloof—*A Name You Can Trust*." I wanted my first and last name in the slogan because I have a somewhat uncommon last name, and it seems to stick.

The idea is to get people used to your name or your slogan. Whatever you put more weight on, just make it something you will not have to change in the future. If you sell residential real estate now but may get into commercial property in the future, don't make a slogan that focuses on residential property. Keep it basic so if you change your specialty, you can carry the same slogan. Lastly, keep your slogan short and sweet. People won't read more than a short sentence at first glance.

Your slogan should be incorporated into virtually every aspect of your marketing. If you can, include your slogan on your business cards, and definitely print your slogan on your envelope and letterhead for your farm and FSBO mailings.

Your Mission Statement

A business just isn't a business without a mission statement. For your website, personal office web page, or for your resume, you'll need to provide a mission statement. A mission statement shouldn't be more than a couple of sentences long. Your mission statement needs to communicate these three important elements:

1. Your purpose
2. Your business
3. Your value

Think about what you provide within these guidelines. You can create each part individually, and then incorporate them into one statement. Here is an example:

Your Purpose: To provide quality services
Your Business: Guiding homeowners through transactions
Your Value: Saving clients time and money while building new relationships

Now when you put all of that together, your mission statement would look like this:

To provide quality services guiding homeowners through transactions, saving them time and money while building new relationships.

So what is your personal mission statement? Create a unique mission statement that identifies your qualities.

CHAPTER 11

Putting Your For-Sale Signs to Work

Success depends on your backbone, not your wishbone.

—Unknown Author

FSBO Fact

Almost two-thirds of agent-assisted sellers and buyers said they *definitely* would use the same agent again in future transactions, and another fifth said they would *probably* use the same agent.

Source: National Association of Realtors®, *Profile of Home Buyers and Sellers,* 2006.

Listings are the backbone of this business. They'll contribute more to your sales than any other approach. Any top producer will share this same thought. Once you start building your listing bank, you'll notice that buyer calls from your signs will start to increase. This is only natural. The more signs in front of properties the more buyer calls you'll receive. So what do you do with the buyers that call? Do you refer them to someone else?

Converting Calls into Sales

You don't get paid if you don't go to work. Furthermore, if you don't try to work with buyers you'll lose out on sales. I'm not saying to *focus* on buyers. This book is actually about focusing on sellers, FSBOs to be exact. But you can't reject buyers that call you. That would be throwing money down the drain. These are people who evidently want to *buy.* It's your job to decide how serious they are and whether they are worth your time.

Three Types of Buyers

In this business we refer to the three types of buyers as "A," "B," and "C" buyers. The breakdown is as follows:

- *"A" buyers* are ready and able to buy *now,* and they will buy very soon. If you find out that you're working with an "A" buyer, keep them as your client. They will put money into your pocket.

- *"B" buyers* are ready and able to buy now, but are not in a rush to do so. They may be pre-approved and ready to move, but they are just very picky and want to see every home in town before they make their decision. If you don't have any irons in the fire, work with them. If you want to put your time to better use and focus on your listings, refer them to another agent for a referral fee.

- *"C" buyers* usually end up being a waste of time. These are buyers who say they want to buy a home but maybe don't have their finances lined up yet, or want to offer half price for everything that's on the market. Stop yourself from wasting too much time on buyers who are not serious about buying, and refer them to other agents. If you're lucky, you'll get a referral fee if buyers you've referred actually buy something through the agent you referred them to.

Converting Buyers into Sales

Converting buyers into sales requires you to adopt a few techniques. Even if some of you already know this information, review it again because it is crucial for your success in converting leads.

Do Not Give Out the Address!!

So many new agents will work the phone like this:

Buyer: "Hi, I'm calling about your ad in the paper about a home by the park."
Agent: "Yes, how can I help you with that?"
B: "What is the address of that property?"
A: "555 W. Belmont."
B: "[CLICK!]"

I don't care what it takes, just do not give out the address. You are only giving them a reason to hang up and never call you back again. And if they said they're going to call you back . . . *THEY'RE LYING!*

Meet them in the office. Don't *offer* to meet them, *tell them* you'll meet them. Offering to meet them will only give them an opening for a "No" response. Get their phone number and give them yours.

If they insist on you giving them the address, here's a good technique to use. Tell them they probably won't buy the house that they're calling in about. But, wait, you want them to buy the house they're calling about . . . *right?* Here is some dialogue to help you understand what I mean:

> **Buyer:** "Hi, I'm calling about your ad in the paper about a home by the park."
>
> **Agent:** *"What a great home, my name is [Your Name], who am I speaking with?"*
>
> **B:** "Gary."
>
> **A:** *"Gary, in case we get disconnected, is the number you called me from the best number to reach you?"*
>
> **B:** "Yes."
>
> **A:** *"Good, how can I help you, Gary?"*
>
> **B:** "What is the address of that property?"
>
> **A:** *"Well, I'd like to give you the address but before I do, is it okay if I ask you a couple of questions to see if this property is right for you?"*
>
> **B:** "I just want the address."

A: *"Gary, the reason why I would like to ask you some questions first is because you probably won't end up buying this property?"*

B: "Why is that?"

A: *"Well, studies show that 95 percent of buyers don't buy the home they call in on. The reason I'm telling you this is because I really want to be sure that this is a home that is right for you before you drive all the way to the property and find out that it's not. Does that make sense?"*

B: "Well, I guess."

[You then ask the buyer some basic questions about what they're looking for and let them know if this home has it.]

A: *"How many bedrooms are you looking for, Gary?"*

B: "Three."

A: *"This one only has two. . . . If everything else in this home was right for you, would you consider buying a home with two bedrooms?"*

B: "No, I need three bedrooms."

A: *"So, aren't you glad I didn't give you the address?"*

B: "Yeah."

A: *"I would like to help you find you the perfect home in an ideal neighborhood. Let's meet tomorrow and talk about finding you that home. Does that sound good?"*

B: "Yeah, that sounds like a good idea."

A: *"I have 4 P.M. open tomorrow, or would 6 P.M. work better for you?"*

This is an effective way to get them into the office. Remember, do not hesitate to ask for the appointment.

Do You Have an Agent?

This should be the first question you ask a buyer who calls you. You don't want to work hard selling a buyer on a listing for ten minutes and then at the end find out that they have an agent. You'll essentially do that agent's job for them.

If they say that they have an agent, ask them if they are actively working with that agent. The reason for this is that many buyers will say that they have an agent just to avoid you claiming them as your clients. If they say that they are not actively working with their agent, ask for their agent's information so you can e-mail the agent the listing that they inquired about. Now, if they don't have the agent's information, chances are they are bluffing. Don't call them out on their bluff but ask them, nonchalantly, whether they would like you to show them some properties.

Are They Able to Buy?

Screen the buyers to find their buying ability. Ask if they are qualified for a mortgage and for how much. Ask them how long they have been searching for a home. And, finally, ask them what their timeline is to purchase. If they aren't qualified for a loan, have a loan officer you work with contact them to qualify them. Then you'll have more control over the transaction when they buy.

Are You Speaking with the Decision Maker?

In any sales setting you find yourself in, make sure you are working with the decision maker. If you don't know who the decision maker is, just ask, "Are you the decision maker?" If they say no, then ask to speak with that person. It's that simple. If you are not speaking with the decision maker, you're spinning your wheels. Know whom you have to win over and find that out as soon as possible.

They Probably Won't Buy That Home

Buyers rarely buy the home they call in on, as you've seen demonstrated in our last dialogue example. You have about a 5 percent chance that the buyer who calls you will be the buyer who buys your property. Make sure you know the inventory of homes that are for sale around all of your listings. By questioning the buyer, you should be able to convert them to a nearby listing that ideally fits what they're looking for. Meet them at a property that fits their needs and start from there. Once you're face to face with them, get to know them and set up the next date for showings.

Don't Sell the Home Over the Phone

No buyer will be sold on a home over the phone. Keep this in mind, real estate agents don't sell property, property sells property. Over the phone, focus on setting up a time to meet. Once you get them into the home, then you can put your sales skills into action to lead them in the right direction.

Sign Call Dialogue

When you have multiple For-Sale signs with your phone number on them, you'll soon be getting buyers calling you. Sign calls are an excellent source of leads but you'll get the good with the bad. Here are some tips to turn your sign calls into appointments.

Introduce Yourself

Introducing yourself, in essence, puts them in the position to introduce themselves. Here is some dialogue that demonstrates what I mean:

> **Buyer:** "Hi, I'm calling about the house for sale on Sunnyside."
>
> **Agent:** "What a great property. I'm [Your Name], who am I speaking with?"
>
> **B:** "This is Ms. Jones."
>
> **A:** "Ms. Jones, I'd love to tell you all about the property you're calling about. But before I get started, is the number that you're calling from the best way to reach you?"
>
> [I assume you have caller ID.]
>
> **B:** "Yes, this is my phone number."

Do They Have an Agent?

Ask if they are working with an agent. If they are, you can exchange the following dialogue:

> **Agent:** "Are you working with an agent?"
>
> **Buyer:** "Yes, we are."

A: *"Well, I'd be glad to help you with basic information, but it would be best to have your agent call me directly so I can get you into this property as soon as possible."*

Qualify Them

Qualifying a buyer clears out all of the unknowns that may prevent you from going forward with a buyer. Make sure you "sharpen the saw" and get these unknowns out of the way, first and foremost. The qualifying method is going to require a different approach. You just can't question the buyer to death without giving them back something that they want. They'll just hang up. Don't give out the price and don't give out the address. What you do is answer their question with a question, as illustrated earlier in the dialogue with Gary. Here are some examples:

Buyer: *"What is the price of the house?"*
Agent: *"What price range are you pre-approved to buy in?"*
B: *"The $300,000 to 350,000 range."*
A: *"Well, you fit right in. What type of home are you searching for?"*

Build Rapport

To build rapport, use the same techniques we just discussed. Answer a question with a question to build a relationship with the buyer. Try to find characteristics in common with your prospect. This will lead you to close for the appointment. For example:

Buyer: *"I'm looking for a brick bungalow."*

Agent: *"Those are very fine homes. How long have you been looking for a bungalow?"*

B: *"About three months now."*

A: *"I have been involved in many bungalow transactions. I find that the main feature buyers love about a bungalow is the layout, wouldn't you agree?"*

Close for the Appointment

Now here's your opportunity to close for the appointment:

Agent: *"If I were to find you a bungalow that was just right for you and for the right price, would you be ready to buy?"*

Buyer: *"That's a possibility."*

A: *"Well, I'm available to show you this home today at 3 P.M., or would 6 P.M. work better for you?"*

Once you start building your listing inventory, you'll find the need to use these dialogue examples. Converting buyer calls into sales can exponentially increase your business per year. You never know, you may get a buyer who falls in the 5-percent of buyers who actually end up buying the home they call about. It happens. And when it does, it pays big.

Putting a "Sold" Rider on Pending Listings

The best way for you to prove to the world that your services are effective is to put a "sold" rider on your properties. When neighbors in the area see a "sold" rider on your For-Sale sign, they'll know that you did your job and sold the home that you were hired to market. This is a successful sale in front of their face and in their area. This is the absolute best local marketing you can carry out.

CHAPTER 12

Servicing Your Listings

Try not to become a man of success. Rather become a man of value.

—ALBERT EINSTEIN

FSBO Fact

Eighty-four percent of sellers used an agent or broker to sell their home, and only 12 percent sold without professional assistance.

SOURCE: National Association of Realtors®, *Profile of Home Buyers & Sellers*, 2006.

In this chapter we'll go over ways to effectively service and sell your listing inventory. Once you acquire an inventory that will keep you busy, you'll need to keep your sellers satisfied and ultimately sell your listings, one by one.

How to Professionally Service Your Listings

The main idea behind providing good service is to keep your clients satisfied while doing everything possible to sell the listing. Furthermore, when you sell a listing and satisfy a client, you build your referral base. More on building a referral base in Chapter 13.

Seller Updates

All too often I hear stories from FSBOs about the bad experiences they had with their previous agent. The main reason why sellers are dissatisfied with their previous agents is that the agents never called them with updates or follow-ups. And we wonder why they're trying to sell FSBO. Put yourself in their shoes and you'll understand why sellers need to know what's going on with the sale of their *largest investment.* Call your sellers at least once or twice a week. This is probably the biggest investment that they have. When they are not sure what is happening with it, they'll get upset. Calling your sellers with weekly or bi-weekly updates will keep you on a comfortable level with them. Not all sellers would like to be called every week. In that case, when you're at the listing presentation, establish how often they'd like an update call.

Have Something to Talk About

Make sure you have something to talk about with your sellers. If there has been no activity on their home, tell them that, but make sure you have something else to tell them as well. Check to see what recently came on the market and what recently went under contract in the area. This will give some valuable insight as to why there has been no activity on their home. If you *did* have activity on the home, let the seller know the level of interest you were able to perceive from the agent or the buyers. You can also discuss what has been happening with the local housing market. Whether the market has been slow or whether it's booming, they'll appreciate the fact that you kept them informed firsthand.

Schedule Showings Yourself

Call your seller to schedule showing requests you receive from other agents yourself. Many offices have secretaries who will call your seller to schedule showings when you don't have to be at the property in person to show it. Having your office secretaries call your sellers to book showings sends a message that you are giving your work to someone else. When you make that call yourself, you will not only be providing the sellers with personalized service, but you are able to give them an update on their home, such as market activity or feedback from the previous showing. If you are selling a property that is currently vacant, there would of course be no need to call your seller to set up showings. Just have your office give the showing agent instructions on how to get in. Do what is best for each situation.

Record Your Showing Appointments

Record your scheduled showing appointments in a log book. Especially when you start racking up listings, you'll need to keep track of all of your showing records for following up and for accountability reasons. If an agent leaves the lights on and the doors open at one of your listings, you'll have a good idea of whom to call and reprimand. For an example of a showing log template, see Appendix C.

Follow Up with Showings

Even if you are familiar with this topic, chances are you don't practice it. Many real estate agents will let other agents shop their listing with buyers and not follow up to ask them how the buyers liked it. Feedback is important, not only to satisfy your sellers' curiosity, but also to help you gauge what the market is saying about the listing. You won't know your listing is overpriced if no one tells you it is.

Get Constructive Feedback

Ask the showing agent for constructive criticism. This is an opportunity for the agent to tell you the good along with the bad. This information could assist you in getting a much needed price reduction from your seller. The most useful feedback is the bad feedback, such as the paint color being tacky, the dog or cat smell being overwhelming, or it being too cold or hot in the house. Make the seller aware of what feedback you received, because these are often areas that you can get the seller to take care of. This type of feedback is critical to help you sell the listing.

You can make it easy for the showing agent to follow up by sending them an e-mail with a questionnaire for them to answer. Send the e-mail the day of the showing, so the feedback comments are still fresh in their minds.

Open Houses

A great way to let your seller know that you're working hard for them is to hold an open house. Not only is this an excellent opportunity to acquire leads, but if you've been egging your seller for a price reduction, an open house could give you the ammunition you need to get it done. A lackluster or zero turnout at an open house, especially for the second or third time, is an indication of the market reaction to the price of the property. An overpriced listing will bring few or no buyers. The open house will hopefully help convince your seller to realize what needs to be done: *a price reduction!*

When holding an open house, have a sign-in sheet. Make sure there is a space for their name, address, and phone number. If you have activity at your open house, then follow up the next day with the open house attendees. That way, when you call your seller, you can give them the turnout figure and the buyers' remarks about the property.

Partner Up with a Loan Officer

Another good idea is to call a loan officer and ask them to sit your open house with you. A loan officer can pre-qualify buyer leads for you on the spot. When you get buyer leads through the door, it's nice to tell your seller that a loan officer was ready to qualify them for the loan.

Put Your Fax Machine to Work

Advertising your open houses to local real estate offices can really help to boost your turnout. Use a unique approach to your open house advertising, through your fax machine.

Most fax machines have the option to program multiple fax numbers into one group. For example, say you want to fax the closest twenty-five real estate offices an open house advertisement the morning of the open house. What you can do is program the fax numbers of those twenty-five offices into one group. When you're ready to fax, the fax machine will automatically dial and send each fax one by one, until every flyer is sent. This is a great tool that goes to work for you while you're getting your open house staged and ready. If you are purchasing a fax machine, buy a fax machine that has a group fax option. Each fax machine is different, so follow the instructions that come with your fax to carry out this task.

Broker's Open

A broker's open is an open house (usually during the week) that invites other agents and brokers to the property. Holding a broker's open will give you feedback directly from the industry experts about the pricing and sales potential of the property that you're selling. Here are some ideas on how to get agents and brokers to come to your broker's open.

- Have a raffle drawing to win a prize.
- Offer a free catered lunch at the broker's open.
- Have a wine and champagne party at your broker's open (usually conducted in the early evening).
- Give out gift certificates to a local coffee shop.

If your sellers have not listened when open house buyers are saying the price is too high, maybe they'll listen to the industry experts. A broker's open provides great ammunition toward your effort to get a price reduction.

Revising Your CMA

Do you have a listing that has been sitting on the market for three months or more? Maybe it's time to see how the market has changed since you took the listing. Every three months that your listing sits on the market, give your seller a revised market analysis. Sometimes comparable homes will sell within a three-month time span. That will influence the overall market value and competition of your listing. The market is constantly changing, so keep a close eye on it. This technique will be especially important when you are in a declining housing market, a buyer's market, or when you're trying to persuade your seller to change the price.

Taking Multiple Photos

If you don't own a digital camera, buy one. These are almost as important as your cell phone. When you get a listing, take as many photos as your local MLS system will allow you to upload. Most MLS systems allow several photos to be hosted on your listing page. If you have a digital camera, you can upload these images the very second your listing goes into the system. Many buyers will not even look at a listing unless it has interior photos. And if you're in a buyer's market, multiple pictures are not even an option, but a must. You can also use these photos for your brochures. This will let your sellers know that you are leaving no stone left unturned.

Making Professional Brochures

When other agents show your listing, it's nice to have the buyers look at a professionally prepared, custom brochure as they walk through the home. These are usually placed in a visible spot when entering the home. Many MLS websites have a brochure template for you to work with. All you have to do is fill in the information and up-load your photos. You can go a step further and include the neighborhood statistics in your property brochure.

Getting MLS Training: Using Reverse Prospecting

I'm sure your local MLS office offers training on how to best utilize the MLS and its features. You'll be surprised at how much more you can do with these common programs than you are currently aware of. Many MLS systems offer statistics that show how many agents have e-mailed your listing to their clients and, at the same time, show the level of interest those buyers responded with. This is an excellent gauge of the sales potential of your listing. Showing off this knowledge will delight your sellers. The fact that you have a technological advantage over other agents can really make a difference. You can also contact the agent who received a response from their buyer about your list-ing. This is called reverse prospecting. You can e-mail the agent saying, "Hi, I noticed that you have a buyer interested in my listing on Grace Street. The property is easy to show, when can we get you in?" This is a great sign of things to come for the technology involved in the real estate industry. Utilize this information and really impress your sellers.

Sending Mass E-Mail Flyers

A mass e-mail flyer is a digital advertisement of your listing for sale that is e-mailed to virtually every agent in your surrounding area with an e-mail address. How does it work? Well, there are two ways of doing it.

1. *Subscribe to an e-flyer service.* E-flyer services will give you the basic templates for constructing your flyer. Then all you do is submit the flyer over the Internet, pay a one-time or monthly fee, and it will be e-mailed to virtually every agent in your region. These can be annoying if you receive them in your inbox every day. In a way they lose their personal touch once it becomes a mass mailer. For some E-flyer resources see Appendix A.

2. *Make your own e-flyer.* You can create your own e-flyers and e-mail them out yourself. It takes time but you can make them more specific to agents who work in the area of the property. Making your own e-flyers also comes across as more personal, giving you better odds that the agent will open the e-mail instead of sending it to the junk box.

Here is how you do it. Go onto the MLS and look up offices in the nearby area of the property for which you are creating an e-flyer. Click on each agent one by one and copy and paste their e-mail address onto the e-mail you are sending. You can then personalize the subject of the e-mail how you wish. The more specific your message the better, such as: "Any agents have buyers for a Portage Park bungalow?"

Mailing Proof of Advertisements

If you publish advertisements of your listings in newspapers or magazines, make copies for your sellers. Mail your seller a copy of their home in the local paper that you promised to publish their ad in. You can also print out the ads from major websites that feature their home and mail those to them as well. For the rare sellers who don't have access to the Internet or just don't know how to navigate it, mail them a copy every time their ad goes into the paper. This is just proof that you are fulfilling your promise to them.

CHAPTER 13

Building a Referral Base

We tend to live up to our expectations.

—Earl Nightingale

FSBO Fact

The biggest problem areas for FSBOs are in getting the right price, preparing a home for sale, and understanding and completing paperwork.

Source: National Association of Realtors®,
Profile of Home Buyers & Sellers, 2006.

According to the NAR's 2006 *Profile of Home Buyers & Sellers,* 40 percent of sellers choose an agent who was recommended to them by a friend, neighbor, or family member. It also costs eight times more to gain a new client than to retain an old one. As you can see, transitioning from prospecting FSBOs to working solely through referrals has great benefits. The ultimate goal in the real estate business is to get to a point where your business comes solely from referrals. Referrals are some of the best leads you can get in this business.

80/20 Rule

The 80/20 rule in real estate states that 80 percent of your business should come from current clients and 20 percent of your business should come from new clients. In the beginning, this won't be the case, but it should be your goal for the mid- to long-term. Soon after you begin closing on your converted FSBO listings, you'll start a referral base. Treat these clients well, because you'll need to rely on them for future sales in order for your referral base to succeed down the road.

Keeping Your Clients Forever

The popular saying, "Where there are friends, there is wealth," holds true for the friends and clients you will make throughout your career in real estate. Treat your clients as you treat your good friends, and keep them forever. If you do, you'll have a wealthy future.

Stay in Touch

Send a letter, a holiday greeting card, or give a follow-up call to all of your past clients. Do this to show them you're still in business. Call them a few times per year. Stay their agent for life and milk them for referrals.

Ask for Referrals

When you contact your past clients make sure you ask for referrals. Don't be shy. Mail them extra business cards with a letter and include a Post-it Note that says, "Pass these out to people you know of that are buying or selling." When you get a referral from one of your clients, send them a gift. Reward them for their thoughtfulness and you'll receive more referrals in return.

Make Them Proud

If you want your past clients to refer you to their friends and family, they'll have to be sure that you won't make them look foolish. Give them a reason to refer you. If they are confident that you'll exceed their friends or family's expectations then they'll take pride in referring you. Providing the best service requires that you possess these qualities:

- *Energy.* Be packed with positive energy. This will show that you have passion for your career.

- *Action.* Get the job done. This involves staying on top of the transaction and updating the sellers with major milestones. Prove to the seller that you are always available simply by answering your phone every time they call you. Give your seller updates often. And always show that you are up for the job, whatever that job may demand from you.

- *Quality.* Quality is achieved by hard work. Many sellers want an aggressive, hard-working agent.

Show that you are a quality agent by doing what it takes to meet their needs.

- *Exceeding Expectations.* Offer your services in a way that they wouldn't expect. Give them a gift at closing. Run paperwork errands for them. Just show that you're willing to do whatever it takes to exceed their expectations.
- *Being Their Resource.* You should have many quality tested attorneys, mortgage brokers, banks, and home improvement contractors to refer to your clients. You can also be their resource for local restaurants and recreation in specific neighborhoods. This demonstrates your extensive knowledge of the neighborhood and shows that you are experienced.

Mailing Your Past Clients

It is important to devote some time to keeping your past clients; because you are already their agent, they will use you again. Calling past clients is a great way for you to stay in their mind. But what if they forget about you in the meantime? To be the most efficient when working with your past clients, you'll have to physically stay in touch or at least keep your name in front of them. This would require actually visiting them in person or mail them stuff.

Ten Great Mailing Ideas for Past Clients

1. *Mail a letter.* Send a hand-written letter to your past clients. Let them know how you've been and what's going on in the market. Not only will this be harder to throw out than junk mail, but it will be personal.

2. *Send holiday cards.* Buy holiday cards from a store; don't use your office or company cards. You'll want to be as personal as you can be. Sign each card and hand-address each envelope. Include some business cards in each envelope for referrals to friends and family.

3. *Mail local newsletters.* If you can, mail your past clients a newsletter specifically about the area they live in. This will keep them in the loop with the local housing market. And, since you provided the information, they'll go to you if they should want to know more.

4. *Send calendars.* Calendars get you onto a homeowner's wall or fridge for a whole year. Think about how many times people visit their fridge. Calendar magnets are also very effective and useful. These are also good for monthly farm mailings.

5. *Give them gifts.* Mail your clients a personalized gift. This is a wonderful show of appreciation. Not only that, but what a great conversation topic with friends, family, and neighbors. Everyone will want

you as their agent if they can receive a nice surprise gift every so often. Some gift ideas are personalized coffee mugs, pens, Post-it Notes with your name and info on it, etc. Some of these can be rather expensive, so make sure you have the room for it in your budget.

6. *Advertise on billboards and benches.* These are great for name reinforcement over the long run. Billboards are quite expensive, so a more affordable alternative would be bus stop benches. Advertising on a bus stop bench gets you a ton of publicity. It's also ideal if you can get a bus stop bench in your farm area. You'll need at least a year's lease on this type of advertising to make it work for you.

7. *Give them a picture of their home.* When you sell a home, keep a record of the MLS picture on file. Then, let's say, within six months to a year later, mail your past clients the picture of what their home looked like when they first bought it. Put the picture in a frame with your name and info printed on it (tastefully), and give this to them as a keepsake gift. How nice would that be? They'll definitely be touched by this and remember you.

8. *Call clients on holidays.* Whether it's your current clients or past clients, one way to keep them close is to call them and wish them a happy holiday. To many, the holidays are emotional times for family

togetherness. A call with your personal greeting can go a long way.

9. *Take your clients out to lunch.* Surprise your clients with a letter stating that you would like to take them out to lunch some day soon, or send them a gift card from a nice lunch restaurant. This shows your loyalty to them, and in return you'll get their loyalty.

10. *Let them in on your production in their area.* If you get listings or sales or have been doing CMAs in past clients' neighborhoods, tell them. They'll feel like they know more about what is happening in their area than the neighbors, and they'll like that. Plus, maybe they'll know of someone who is buying or selling in their area and can refer them to you.

The Automated Referral System

There are companies out there that will do most of your follow-up work for you. You simply sign your client up with this system at closing, pay a one-time fee, and they'll take care of your client follow-ups for three to five years. They'll mail newsletters, greeting cards, and yearly calendars. It's a great investment, and what's even better—*it's automated!*

Belonging to Something

When you belong to something like, say, a country club or a gym, you'll build relationships with your fellow members. This is an excellent way to generate referrals. Here are seven ideas for meeting new people in group-style settings:

1. *Throw a party.* Invite clients and friends to a catered wine and dinner party on you. This will bring you closer to your clients. And what do your dinner guests all have in common? You! The talk of the party will probably be you, which is good. They'll share the experiences they had working with you, and they'll go home ready to spread the referrals to everyone they know.

2. *Join a gym.* Not only is it a good idea to belong to a gym for physical and health reasons, but it's a great way to meet new people who are also members.

3. *Play golf.* Golf, which is a very social sport, has long been considered the sport of the elite. So chances are you'll be mingling with homeowners. Where there are homeowners, there is business.

4. *Attend church.* Belonging to a church is a great way to promote yourself. Church members typically feel comfortable with referrals from their fellow church members.

5. *Get involved in your local government.* Local politics or neighborhood associations are groups that are directly tied to the good will of the neighborhood in which you reside. This is an excellent way to show—not only to neighborhood prospects but to the governing organizations that run the local economy—that you are serious about helping residents in the area.

6. *Sponsor a local team.* Many children's sports teams accept sponsor donations. In return you may get your name across the back of their jerseys or helmet. Or you can be listed as a sponsor in their publications. The parents of these children will definitely think highly of you and keep you in mind when buying or selling a home.

7. *Get a hobby.* A hobby such as marathon running, dancing, or even a chess club can help you meet new potential future clients.

Earning a solid referral stream takes patience. Over time, if you follow these tips, you'll set the stage for a successful referral career. Work hard, work smart, and keep at it until your goals are achieved.

APPENDIX A

Resources

Your FSBO Career Resources

Suggested Reading:

Kenneth W. Edwards, *Your Successful Real Estate Career* (New York: AMACOM, 2006).

Tom Hopkins, *Mastering the Art of Selling Real Estate* (New York: Penguin Group, 2004).

Darryl Davis, *How to Become a Power Agent in Real Estate* (New York: McGraw-Hill, 2002).

Internet Resources

Real Estate Audio Sales Training CDs:
www.floydwickmanteam.com
www.nightingale.com
www.tomhopkins.com

Drip-Marketing Sites:
www.proautoresponder.com
www.intersend.com

Realtor Benefits/Lead Providers:
www.eneighborhoods.com

Photo/Name Sign Rider:
www.photosignriders.com

Personalized Printing Company (print on anything!):
www.4imprint.com

Agent Marketing and Stationary Resource:
www.merrillcorp.com

Magnetic Calendars:
www.realestatecalendars.com
www.magnetstreet.com

FSBO Lead Provider Services:
www.landvoice.com
www.fsbohotsheet.com
www.fsboleads.com
www.fsboleader.com
www.fsboleadsusa.com

Do Not Call List:
www.donotcall.gov

Agent Website Builder Services:
www.tourrealestateinc.com
www.agentproducer.com
www.rapidlistings.com

FSBO Statistics:
www.realtor.org/research.nsf/pages/fsbofacts

Field Guide to Working FSBOs:
www.realtor.org/libweb.nsf/pages/fg210

E-Mail Mass Flyers:
www.electronicflyerco.com
www.emailflyerads.com
www.sharperagent.com
www.fastemailflyers.com

APPENDIX B

FSBO Facts

It Pays to Use an Agent

In 2006, the typical FSBO sold for $187,200, compared to $247,000 for agent-assisted home sales. As you can see, this is compelling evidence that using an agent opposed to selling by owner pays big dividends.

Using an Agent vs. Selling FSBO	Percent Price Gain Using an Agent
2006	+ 32 percent
2005	+ 16 percent
2004	+15.4 percent

SOURCE: All data in Appendix B are from the National Association of Realtors®, *Profile of Home Buyers & Sellers, 2004, 2005, and 2006.*

Why Go FSBO?

The main reason sellers choose to go FSBO is to save on the commission. Although that reason is declining, it still outweighs other reasons significantly.

Reasons Sellers Choose to Go FSBO	2004	2005	2006
Commission savings	61 percent	53 percent	51 percent
Selling to a friend, relative, or neighbor	17	22	22
Buyers contacted seller	9	9	12
Avoid dealing with agents	6	8	8
Seller has real estate license	2	2	2
Agent unable to sell home	2	3	3
Couldn't find an agent	1	N/A	1
Other	2	3	2

Small Towns Have Most FSBOs

The highest percentage of FSBOs are located in small towns and in rural areas.

Percentage of home sales
that are FSBO, by area type   *Percent*

Small towns	17
Rural areas	16
Suburbs	11
Urban areas	11
Resorts	10

FSBOs in Decline

Not factoring in FSBOs who know their buyer, FSBOs overall are on the decline.

FSBO & agent-assisted sales	2004	2005	2006
All FSBO	14 percent	13 percent	12 percent
Seller knew buyer	5	5	5
Seller did not know buyer	10	8	7
Agent-assisted	82	85	84
Other	4	2	3

Most Difficult Task for FSBO Sellers

Getting the right price	11 percent
Understanding the paperwork	16 percent
Preparing/fixing up home for sale	18 percent
Attracting potential buyers	9 percent

Having enough time to devote to all
aspects of the sale   9 percent

FSBO Methods Used to Market Home

Yard sign	51 percent
Friends/neighbors	53 percent
Newspaper ad	31 percent
Open house	29 percent
Listing on the Internet	22 percent

APPENDIX C

Sample Forms

Sample Showing Log

Phone:	Time:	Name:
Address:	Company:	ID:

Phone:	Time:	Name:
Address:	Company:	ID:

Phone:	Time:	Name:
Address:	Company:	ID:

Phone:	Time:	Name:
Address:	Company:	ID:

Phone:	Time:	Name:
Address:	Company:	ID:

Phone:	Time:	Name:
Address:	Company:	ID:

Phone:	Time:	Name:
Address:	Company:	ID:

Phone:	Time:	Name:
Address:	Company:	ID:

Figure C-1. Sample showing log.

Sample Resume

[YOUR NAME HERE]

WHY SELLERS PREFER ME OVER THE COMPETITION

Honorable Achievements:

Award winning producer in 2005 and 2006 for highest office production.

Proud member of the Chicago, Illinois, and National Association of Realtors and honor the Realtor® code of ethics.

Real estate is my life. I have total devotion to this career. When you love your profession...*you're good at it!*

MY AGGRESSIVE STRATEGY TO MARKET YOUR HOME

- **VERBAL CANCELLATION LISTING AGREEMENTS...CANCEL ANYTIME...AND PAY $0.**
- Ads in *6* Newspapers including the Tribune, Polish, Spanish, and Neighborhood papers, I put this in writing for.
- 600 Real estate websites including the most visited websites for buyers.
- Multiple Listing Service (MLS).
- Open houses every Sunday (If desired).
- Yard sign w/name rider and cell phone number for efficient buyer leads.
- Direct mail advertising your home.
- Home warranty options.
- Contact our clientele database for buyers already in the system.
- Brochures distributed to high traffic areas.
- Competitive commission schedule.
- **And...HARD WORK... LOYAL WORK...HONEST WORK...FULL TIME...7 DAYS A WEEK!**

Figure C-2. Sample resume.

Wonder how much your home is
WORTH?

FREE Over-the-phone Market Analysis!

Call [Your Name]
Realtor®
[Your Number]

[Company Name]
[Company Address]

FREE INSTANT CMA! CALL [YOUR NAME/NUMBER] [YOUR COMPAMY]

Figure C-3. Sample over-the-phone CMA ad with tear-off stubs.

Sample Over-the-Phone CMA Ad with Tear-Off Stubs

In places where it is difficult to leave flyers or business cards, ads with tear-off stubs can be an easy solution. As shown in the example of an over-the-phone CMA ad in Figure A-3, these tear-off stubs are convenient when placing advertisements in public places. Include the tear-off stubs at the bottom of your one-page ad. Just precut the perforated lines so that prospects can easily tear off your information on the go.

Index

About the Author

This book contains honest accounts from real estate agent John Maloof, a top producer with Century 21 and winner of five awards for his production. Enclosed are the proven techniques that John used to make a six-figure income in his first year as a real estate agent. With no previous sales and no referrals, John used the FSBO market to acquire all of his sales.

Look for These Exciting Real Estate Titles at www.amacombooks.org/go/realestate

A Survival Guide for Buying a Home by Sid Davis $17.95

A Survival Guide for Selling a Home by Sid Davis $15.00

Are You Dumb Enough to Be Rich? by G. William Barnett II $18.95

Everything You Need to Know Before Buying a Co-op, Condo, or Townhouse by Ken Roth $18.95

Make Millions Selling Real Estate by Jim Remley $18.95

Mortgages 101 by David Reed $16.95

Mortgage Confidential by David Reed $16.95

Real Estate Investing Made Simple by M. Anthony Carr $17.95

Real Estate Presentations That Make Millions by Jim Remley $18.95

The Complete Guide to Investing in Foreclosures by Steve Berges $17.95

The Consultative Real Estate Agent by Kelle Sparta $17.95

The First-Time Homeowner's Survival Guide by Sid Davis $16.00

The Home Buyer's Question and Answer Book by Bridget McCrea $16.95

The Landlord's Financial Tool Kit by Michael C. Thomsett $18.95

The Property Management Tool Kit by Mike Beirne $19.95

The Real Estate Agent's Business Planner by Bridget McCrea $19.95

The Real Estate Agent's Field Guide by Bridget McCrea $19.95

The Real Estate Agent's Guide to FSBOs by John Maloof $19.95

The Real Estate Investor's Pocket Calculator by Michael C. Thomsett $17.95

The Successful Landlord by Ken Roth $19.95

Who Says You Can't Buy a Home! by David Reed $17.95

Your Guide to VA Loans by David Reed $17.95

Your Successful Career as a Mortgage Broker by David Reed $18.95

Your Successful Real Estate Career, Fifth Edition by Kenneth W. Edwards $18.95

Available at your local bookstore, online, or call 800-250-5308.

Savings start at 40% on bulk orders of 5 copies or more!

Save up to 55%!

Prices are subject to change.

For details, contact AMACOM Special Sales

Phone: 212-903-8316   E-Mail: SpecialSls@amanet.org